International Social Entrepreneurship

International Social Entrepreneurship

Pathways to Personal and Corporate Impact

J. Mark Munoz

International Social Entrepreneurship: Pathways to Personal and Corporate Impact

Copyright © Business Expert Press, LLC, 2010.

First published in 2010 by
Business Expert Press, LLC
222 East 46th Street, New York, NY 10017
www.businessexpertpress.com

ISBN-13: 978-1-60649-106-5 (paperback)
ISBN-10: 1-60649-106-7 (paperback)

ISBN-13: 978-1-60649-107-2 (e-book)
ISBN-10: 1-60649-107-5 (e-book)

DOI 10.4128/9781606491072

A publication in the Business Expert Press International Business collection

Collection ISSN: 1948-2752 (print)
Collection ISSN: 1948-2760 (electronic)

Cover design by Jonathan Pennell
Interior design by Scribe, Inc.

First edition: June 2010

10 9 8 7 6 5 4 3 2 1

Printed in the United States of America.

Abstract

Social entrepreneurship, or the business practice with the dual bottom line of profit and service, has steadily increased worldwide. While high-profile success cases are notable, business failures are mounting. This book introduces the concept of "international social entrepreneurship" and outlines contemporary challenges and opportunities. Based on real-life cases and internationalization theories, it offers practical instructions for readers to strategically replicate social ventures from one part of the world to another. With the confluence of business globalization and civic-mindedness, an entrepreneurial wave is bound to change the world through its personal and corporate impact.

Keywords

Entrepreneurship, international, social entrepreneurship, social enterprise, international entrepreneurship

Contents

CHAPTER 1

Introduction

No man or woman of the humblest sort can really be strong, gentle, and good, without the world being better for it, without somebody being helped and comforted by the very existence of that goodness.

—Alan Alda

Global business has redefined contemporary ways of life and the conduct of business. It sped up business processes, stimulated innovation, and opened several gateways to prosperity. It intensified cross-border communication and interaction and unified cultures. It set new frameworks for global citizens to engage, collaborate, and find meaning in life.

Globalization has brought the world closer together. It allows everyone to instantaneously gather information and reach out to friends and colleagues in distant places. With cable television, news events from remote corners of the world are broadcasted instantly. With breakthroughs in telecommunications, computers, and the Internet, collaborating with others has been immensely simplified. With advancements in the travel and transport industries, foreign travel, service delivery, and the movement of products have become affordable and accessible to many.

Globalization reconfigured the business paradigm. The heightened integration has been attributed to (a) lower transportation and communication costs arising from sprouting technologies, (b) trade liberalization across several fronts, and (c) more aggressive business endeavors in developed and developing countries.[1] Globalization created a new economic order, and facilitated access to factors of production and new markets, amid heightened global competition.[2] In the view of Pulitzer prize–winning author Thomas Friedman, our world is decidedly "flat."[3]

The global world empowers every individual, corporation, organization, and government entity to make an international impact. Markets, nation-states, and technologies are deeply enmeshed and let everyone reach out to others in a faster, farther, and deeper manner.[4] Through friendships, businesses, and sociocivic pursuits, significant changes are doable in far corners of the world.

Actions pursued by individuals and corporations have changed societies on foreign shores. For instance, Muhammad Yunus's Grameen Bank led to the expansion of microlending that helped millions of struggling poor people in emerging nations. Bill Drayton's Ashoka Foundation supported thousands of entrepreneurs in international locations and consequently improved many communities.

The ability of individuals and corporations to make an international impact is often subject to "push" and "pull" forces. Push forces refer to factors that facilitate the outward, international expansion of companies. Pull forces refer to factors that encourage and draw investments into host countries. Examples of push forces that drive internationalization include home-country policies and trade restrictions, technology, transport and communication efficiencies, Internet and enhanced distribution systems, telecom improvements, economic changes, market forces, and even growing cultural homogenization. Examples of pull forces include attractive resources and policies in host countries that lead to cost benefits, market expansion, operational gain, tax breaks, and relevant incentives. Individuals and organizations seeking to explore opportunities overseas need to deliberate these factors.

Organizations exploring foreign marketplaces have different motives. In their research, authors Mauro Guillen and Esteban Garcia-Canal[5] identified several motivational factors for foreign direct investment by multinational enterprises, including (a) links to resources, (b) access to international markets, (c) overcoming home-country government restrictions, (d) enhancing risk management, (e) moving resources to diversify investment portfolios, (f) following competitors to foreign locations, (g) overcoming trade liberalization and related policies from the home country, (h) access to asset-resource acquisition opportunities, and (i) optimizing use of firm, intangible assets.

Many countries are aggressively working on the "pull" factors in order to attract investment. They are instituting policies, procedures, and guidelines that facilitate global trade. Tariff reductions are a growingly common measure. Many countries seek to ensure that their legal systems, infrastructure, tax laws, and exchange rates are attractive to overseas investors.

The interplay of the push and pull of global forces has redefined the agendas and relationships of individuals, corporations, and countries. For instance, many corporate executives and businessmen engage in outsourcing and creative strategic alliances in emerging markets; multinational corporations scour the world for new opportunities while countries and many governments embrace privatization to attract investments.

Amid heightened global integration and international trade expansion, challenges exist. While many individuals, companies, and governments have benefited from globalization, millions have been left out of the loop. While many have found a gateway to prosperity, millions struggle with poverty, disease, pollution, and other social challenges. The process of globalization is not entirely balanced, and complacency and lack of concern for the welfare of others can lead to more pressing problems in the future. In the view of Professor Russel Botman, globalization tends to spawn individualism and may lead to the loss of community spirit within and among countries.[6] Competitive pressures, motivation for financial gain and survival, and the push for constant excellence may lead to an emphasis on personal gain rather than the needs of the society.

Globalization therefore opens up a new set of questions for its citizens:

1. Has technological breakthrough, international integration, and newfound prosperity enhanced our outlook of the world?
2. With expanded global relationships, have we become more compassionate, caring, or humane than generations before us?
3. As members of the now global community, what have we and our companies contributed?

The success of a society largely rests on the contributions of its members. In recent years, the global community has been fortunate to be a recipient of the gifts of talent and resources from change makers who strive to positively impact the world.

Socially inspired citizens are bringing about notable changes to communities worldwide. Author David Bornstein observed that in the realm of public service, internationalization is taking place in an unprecedented scale, is growingly diverse, and is comprised of dynamic interorganizational alliances that are implementing innovative solutions to social problems.[7] In past decades, civic consciousness and community spirit were awakened in many as a response to events and natural tragedies such as floods, earthquakes, famine, and disease. However, in recent years, involvement in humanitarian causes has expanded through the creation of organizations responding to various forms of self-made misery often created by humankind.

Among the socially oriented citizenry, a distinct group has opted to engage in the practice of social entrepreneurship. Author Alan Fowler defines social entrepreneurship as the "creation of viable socio-economic structures, relations, institutions, organizations and practices that yield and sustain social benefits."[8] The Social Enterprise Alliance defines social enterprises as "organizations that achieve its primary social and environmental mission using business methods."[9] In an email correspondence with Dr. Rebecca Harding, managing director of Delta Economics, she stated, "These organizations are set up to pursue social, community, ethical or environmental goals and redistributes revenues and surpluses to fulfill those goals."[10] Authors Sandra Waddock and James Post describe social entrepreneurs as "private sector citizens who play critical roles in bringing about 'catalytic changes' in the public sector agenda and the perception of social issues."[11] The Ashoka Foundation, a leading social enterprise, characterizes the breed as "practical visionaries" who possess vision, innovation, determination, and long-term commitment to social change.[12] These unique individuals enhance social value, exercise fair and virtuous judgments, and strategically and creatively tap into opportunities that lead to reform.[13]

In recent years, the business world witnessed the emergence of social entrepreneurs. For instance, in the United States, Wendy Kopp founded Teach for America, an organization that provides college students the opportunity to serve communities by becoming teachers in various locations across the country.[14] A company called YouthBuild was formed to help marginalized youths earn diplomas, learn skill sets, and engage in community service by helping build low-cost homes.[15] A nonprofit enterprise known as KaBOOM expanded rapidly and attracted millions of dollars from donors to develop playgrounds for local communities.[16]

While social entrepreneurship has been active in the United States, similar trends are taking place in other parts of the world. In Africa, Martin Fisher and Nick Moon started an organization called KickStart. The company identifies and markets innovative technologies in the region and sells them to local entrepreneurs, thereby providing a win–win scenario where the inventor earns, the businessman makes money, and the community benefits from the innovation.[17] Paul Farmer founded Partners in Health, an organization that provides affordable treatment solutions in addressing health issues in developing countries.[18] In the United Kingdom, a successful social enterprise known as Guide Dogs for the Blind Association (GDBA) breeds and trains Seeing Eye dogs, thereby catering to a social need while gaining profit.[19]

Many social enterprises have taken on creative pursuits with missions that have high community impact. For instance, Divine Chocolate ensures that cocoa purchases for their chocolates are acquired via fair trade;[20] Big Issue is a newspaper company that lets homeless people sell their newspapers;[21] Housing Works runs thrift shops, a book store, and a catering company, among other businesses, to support their mission of fighting AIDS and homelessness;[22] Rubicon uses research, science, and education to support divers, aviators, and researchers worldwide;[23] Community Wealth Ventures provides social enterprise consulting;[24] and Social Enterprise Reporter provides news and reports for the social enterprise and related sectors.[25] There are many other examples engaged in diverse industries. Social enterprises are noted in sectors such as retail, service, and manufacturing; social services; research and consulting; community development; finance; and technology.[26]

While many social enterprises are start-ups, some have been established by proven and tested entrepreneurs. For instance, internationally renowned entrepreneurs, like Jeff Skoll of eBay, Bill Gates of the Microsoft Corporation, and Richard Branson of Virgin Group, engaged in social entrepreneurship after a successful career in industry. Later in life, they responded to a social call by creating ventures that positively impact society. They set up foundations or grant-giving entities that aid international communities, and they support the growth and expansion of social entrepreneurship.

Enterprises that are both socially driven and profit driven are expanding.[27] The concept and practices behind social enterprises are not entirely new. In the United States, elements of social enterprise thinking have been observed in years past and were visible in community activism, civic campaigns, and even political movements.[28] In the United Kingdom, even years ago, sociocivic programs that focused on job creation were observed.[29] At the present time, social entrepreneurship is gaining popularity in the United States and United Kingdom.[30] The number of non-profit organizations exceeds 1 million worldwide and continues to grow. In an e-mail interview with Molly Barker, founder of Girls on the Run, she indicated that "our society is evolving . . . more individuals are learning that external rewards relating to money, prestige, and career are not always gratifying."[31] Furthermore, Robert McEwan, CEO of Medbank pointed out that "lack of grant funding, and the pressure for granting agencies for grantees to be sustainable contributed to the expansion of social entrepreneurship."[32]

There is a growing interest among young entrepreneurs and executives to engage in social entrepreneurship. Leading business schools have integrated social entrepreneurship programs in their curricula. There has been a noticeable increase in socially directed entrepreneurs entering business schools or integrating a social dimension to their business.[33] There are even business plan competitions based on social venture creation.

Research suggests that market factors shape the creation of social enterprises.[34] Social enterprises are sometimes seen as solutions for market or state failures:[35] "Social entrepreneurship is the mechanism by which entrepreneurial solutions are found to social, ethical, welfare or increasingly environmental problems."[36] In the case of philanthropic endeavors, recent trends suggest a growing inclination toward more proactive, participative, and collaborative engagements.[37]

Many social enterprises possess a strong social dimension and utilize a business format to expand their service goals.[38] They appear in diverse organizational forms including charity, not-for-profit, cooperative, sole traders, partnerships, and even limited liability corporations.[39] Hybrid organizational models exist with a broad mix of profit and nonprofit interfaces.[40] Organizational structures include a regular corporation with a product or service specifically directed at a social need, or a company that is profit oriented but engages in an occasional program that responds to a social issue.[41]

The practice of social entrepreneurship may be viewed as an entrepreneurial pursuit with a social intent.[42] It is sometimes called "civic entrepreneurship."[43] Organizations engaged in this practice have a two-pronged mission that combines profit and service[44] and thereby have a "double bottom line" with both economic and social benefits.[45] In some cases, practitioners even aim for a triple bottom line (3BL) and pursue goals that impact "people, planet, and profits."[46]

Social entrepreneurship is heavily anchored on vision formation and a drive toward change.[47] This passion toward change has been evident not only in industrialized locations but also in emerging nations. For instance, in China, a company called Shokay gathered yak products from Tibet and created a fashionable line of clothing, accessories, and home decors that are sold internationally. Their model led to income generation, cultural preservation, sustainable environmental conservation, and community development.[48] In this case, the dynamic vision of founders Carol Chyau and Marie So helped transform several poor communities.

Social entrepreneurs tend to be ordinary individuals who pursue extraordinary missions. They utilize resources on hand to further a unique social agenda.[49] The work of social entrepreneurs is evident in almost any industry—what sets them apart is the innovative approach in which their business is conducted. Social entrepreneurs positively impact society while doing financially well at the same time.[50] Many of them implement unique and innovative models that deviate from past paradigms and that transform societies.

The agenda of social entrepreneurs extend beyond their local communities. Their drive to bring about change leads them to make an impact on individuals and communities in international locations. They are active and high-achieving global citizens that shape the world through an endeavor that balances the quest for profit with social betterment.

There are two types of social entrepreneurs: (a) domestic social entrepreneurs, concerned primarily in dealing with social issues in the local or domestic community, and (b) international social entrepreneurs, concerned with making a social impact in international locations and possibly the entire world.

This book focuses on the practice of international social entrepreneurship (ISE). Those engaged in the practice shall be referred to as "international social entrepreneurs," and the ventures they create will be referred to as "international social enterprises."

The topic of ISE is timely and relevant for eight reasons: (a) there is an extreme need for help and support in many emerging markets in the world, and proactive action from global citizenry is needed; (b) with heightened global integration and expanded organizational reach, businessmen and executives from private corporations, government, and international organizations are geographically positioned to implement socially responsive programs in foreign countries; (c) technological advancements have added ease and convenience in cross-border communication and interaction in foreign locations; (d) media, Internet, interorganizational alliances, friendships and family relations, and the expansion of cross-border contacts and networks have led to heightened awareness and empathy for social issues on foreign shores; (e) as more organizations expand into foreign territories, creative forms of social responsiveness and community collaboration are necessary; (f) with global integration, social challenges such as poverty, disease, and pollution are shared by countries worldwide and require cooperation across different levels and channels; (g) there is a growing shift and interest from traditional, passive charitable giving to more proactive, dynamic, interactive, and entrepreneurial models; and (h) the global world has empowered individuals, companies, and countries to make a positive and lasting international impact that could transform societies.

Through global business, there are several approaches by which ISE could be practiced. For instance, a business executive setting up a factory or business operation in a foreign location may see an opportunity for enhancing the company's corporate image and building goodwill by engaging in, or supporting, an international social enterprise. There are several potential practitioners: companies may find strategic value in integrating a social program component in their global business development efforts in order to improve profitability or brand appeal; partnerships with private companies or government entities in foreign countries may require a social component; entrepreneurs seeking to find a unique niche in the competitive global marketplace may find specialized opportunities in ISE; individuals with excess financial resources, or those looking to find meaning in their lives, may find the practice of ISE appealing; individuals who retire overseas may want to initiate or collaborate in socially oriented initiatives; and spouses or children of company expatriates or entrepreneurs living overseas for extended periods of time may find exciting opportunities in social programs.

Knowledge of ISE is useful to sectors other than business. It is also valuable to governments, think tanks, and international organizations. For instance, governments have initiated measures to attract large, private corporations to their countries. There is an additional need to thoroughly explore modalities in which foreign social enterprises can be attracted. A country that nurtures social enterprises benefits by having several pro-active groups caring for the citizenry. Countries with limited financial resources would be helped by the presence of social enterprises. Think tanks, consulting companies, and international organizations benefit from knowledge of ISE, since the information gathered from social enterprises and cases could set the framework for the creation of favorable and effective policies.

Despite its wide and broad appeal, there is much to be learned about the practice of ISE. In an effort to build a body of knowledge on the practice, this book shall (a) explore stories and cases pertaining to domestic and international social entrepreneurs and their companies, (b) examine business approaches utilized by social entrepreneurs and their companies, and (c) integrate concepts, theories, and strategies pertaining to business enterprise internationalization. Through the combination of gathered information and learned concepts, a new and actionable knowledge base is created. The objective of this book is to further the understanding of ISE and identify practical and viable business practices that are applicable to diverse sectors. The book is written in a concise and easy-to-understand manner so that students and executives from different backgrounds can draw upon the lessons and integrate the learned concepts into their own lines of work.

Concept understanding often starts with a good definition. In defining social entrepreneurship, it is helpful to examine the characteristics of its practitioners—the social entrepreneurs. In gathered literature, social entrepreneurs have been described as possessors of the following attributes.

Proactive. Social entrepreneurs are individuals who see and identify an unmet need in a society and who mobilize manpower and financial and other resources to make a social impact.[51] For instance, the National Foundation for Teaching Entrepreneurship (NFTE) promotes leadership and business skills, focusing on enhancing these skills in young men and women. The organization started as a home-based enterprise and has grown into a multimillion-dollar business through active gathering of corporate donors and support.[52]

Risk takers. Many social entrepreneurs are perceived as risk takers who possess skills and abilities to deliver new concepts and ideas to a wider framework of society.[53] A key attribute for social entrepreneurs is that they should be "risk takers who are willing to stake their reputations and work in difficult environment."[54] Café Direct sells tea and coffee acquired through "fair trade," and the company profits are used to support the training of farmers in the developing world.[55] The path they have chosen is unconventional, difficult, and one that may be viewed as a risky business proposition, but the impact they have made has been profound.

Mission oriented. Social entrepreneurs are characterized as having a predefined mission, engaged in a nonprofit endeavor, being organization-centric, and being stewards of financial resources.[56] Many social ventures build their work around their chosen mission. An essential attribute of a social entrepreneur is "passion for the mission."[57] Greyston Bakery directs its efforts into helping those who have been unemployed for a long period of time.[58] In fact, their guiding principles speak clearly of their goal: "We don't hire people to bake brownies, we bake brownies to hire people."[59]

Focused on societal reform. Many authors perceive social entrepreneurship as heavily anchored on pursuing socially responsive causes. Social entrepreneurs focus on social goals and objectives while implementing their operational strategies,[60] converge business acumen with a social conscience,[61] and pursue methodologies of business, governance, and philanthropy that are anchored on social transformation.[62] They pursue social betterment through a value-added element.[63] Their proposed change initiatives are typically different from past approaches used in dealing with a problem in society.[64] For example, a company called Kiva.org has used the Internet as a medium to facilitate microlending for struggling entrepreneurs in emerging markets.[65] Through their person-to-person, web-based lending approach, they chose a nontraditional yet effective approach to address the issue of poor capital accessibility in emerging nations.

Policy reform catalysts. Some researchers note the key role of societal actors as catalysts for policy reform and enhancement,[66] while others cite several cases where civic-oriented entrepreneurs were instrumental in positive policy changes.[67] "Social entrepreneurs need the ability to influence."[68] For instance, New Schools Network is a nonprofit organization engaged in education reform by funding and supporting initiatives that positively impact public education.[69]

Innovative and adaptive spirit. Social entrepreneurs are precursors of change through the creation of social values, innovation, and parsimonious adaptation,[70] and they exhibit a strong desire to build social capital through concept enhancement, the introduction of new methodologies and technologies, and management systems.[71] For instance, in South Africa, an open-access university was created to (a) provide low-cost, high-scale education models; (b) offer free lectures on various training; (c) accept donations of money and equipment from individuals and companies; (d) allow companies and private benefactors to sponsor students; and (e) provide students the opportunity to participate in running the school.[72]

Entrepreneurial methodologies. Academics and authors observe strong entrepreneurial tendencies among social entrepreneurs. These individuals build on value and strive to gain an operational surplus;[73] they pursue a business-centered approach with the strategic utilization of alliances and partners;[74] and they have skills such as efficient resource mobilization, orientation toward results, and operational efficiency.[75] They have high market sensitivity and revenue-generation abilities[76] and are adept at identifying opportunities in which to create products or services that suit the market.[77] In the United States, a company called Triangle Residential Options for Substance Abusers (TROSA) is a self-sustaining program that helps substance abusers through 2 years of in-house treatment. Participants are involved in entrepreneurial pursuits—such as mowing services and lawn maintenance—that lead to the generation of income.[78]

International orientation. An interest in international and global projects is observed among social entrepreneurs. There is an emergence of internationally directed, civic-oriented actors who operate as noninstitutional bodies and who are transforming the global agenda by engaging in business that addresses important international social issues such as poverty, health, and environment.[79] Simultaneously, socially inspired citizens have introduced innovative programs and policy changes that transformed society. While domestic residents operate some social ventures, there are instances where foreign citizens have played an active role as well. The conveniences brought about by global telecommunication, the Internet, and computer technology have expanded the interest in, and internationalized the practice of, social entrepreneurship. For example, masters-degree students at the Haas Business School at the University of California created a business plan called World of Good, which facilitated the retail sale of art products of women from emerging nations.[80]

In combining the various viewpoints on the subject, international social entrepreneurship, or ISE, can be defined as *a dynamic process undertaken by individuals who are proactive, risk-taking, and mission-oriented leaders who pursue global or internationally directed initiatives that catalyze societal and policy reform through entrepreneurial methodologies that are anchored on innovation and an adaptive spirit.*

There are several benefits associated with social entrepreneurship: (a) the building of economic vitality; (b) the parsimonious pursuit of a mission; (c) the generation of employment; (d) cultivation of morality, equity, and social change; and (e) provision of exemplary models of social responsibility.[81]

Several social enterprises have strong moral or spiritual components that are often absent in traditional business ventures.[82] Aside from aiming to address a wide range of contemporary social issues, social enterprises direct their efforts toward the poor and the underprivileged.[83] For instance, in the United Kingdom, a social enterprise known as Aspire helps and supports the homeless.[84] The founders of KickStart, Nick Moon and Martin Fisher, identified three measures of success for themselves by asking meaningful questions such as the following:

1. Did the people we helped move out of poverty?
2. Can more people take advantage of our introduced approaches?
3. Is the company moving toward self-sufficiency?[85]

In certain instances, vital social issues were addressed and led to widespread attention and action. For instance, in the United States, social efforts that are characterized by wide participation, such as Hands Across America, Earth Day, and Partnership for a Drug-Free America, attract attention to global issues such as hunger and homelessness, neglect of the environment, and drugs.[86] Heifer International is an organization that provides continuous loans to entrepreneurs to stimulate livestock or farming initiatives. In turn, program recipients are expected to pass on their first set of generated assets to another person. The program has touched millions of lives and has expanded to over 100 countries.

In many cases, the initiators of social change are regular citizens who have a strong desire to see reforms materialize, and who have used available resources at their disposal to ensure that reforms take place. Authors

Sandra Waddock and James Post indicate that social entrepreneurs are (a) private citizens rather than public servants, (b) individuals focused on increasing public awareness of social issues, and (c) seekers of solutions through enhanced attention on societal problems.[87]

In the view of author Alan Fowler, motivational forces that spawn sociocivic awareness and action predominantly take place as a result of (a) the precarious state of newly independent nations, (b) repression of value systems arising from colonial rule, (c) the emerging need for support of broad social issues such as environmental degradation, and (d) the opportunity to lend support to nation-building efforts of governments throughout the world.[88] There is growing interest in social entrepreneurship because (a) financial crises cause many to question whether pursuit of wealth is in the society's best interest, (b) social problems and inequalities open up opportunities for finding socially sustainable solutions, and (c) social issues often require "entrepreneurial solutions."[89]

With regard to function, author Mark Pomerantz describes the following characteristics of social enterprises: (a) they are self-sustaining and revenue-generating initiatives, (b) they are sponsored through grants and donations, (c) they take affirmative approaches through client employment generation, (d) they are mission oriented, and (e) they access non-core income streams.[90]

In practicing social entrepreneurship, some organizations create new ventures specifically directed toward a social cause, while others innovate by introducing new organizational structures and fresh paradigms.[91] For instance, a company called Endeavor directed its efforts at providing capital access and nurturing high-impact entrepreneurs, a dire need in many societies.[92] A company called Green-Works provided innovation in the recycling business.[93] This company recycles furniture by having donors dispose of their furniture in a convenient and environmentally friendly manner, and, at the same time, the recycled units are sold to educational institutions and civic organizations at bargain prices.[94]

In many cases, social entrepreneurs provided attention to organizational profitability in order to sustain their ventures and broaden the impact of their social agendas.[95] NFTE grew to a multimillion-dollar enterprise while remaining dedicated to their mission.[96]

In recent years, civic-directed endeavors were formed by spiritually inclined and socioculturally sensitive organizations seeking to make a positive impact in both domestic and international settings.[97] Some of these firms were developed to support social entrepreneurs. For instance, in the United Kingdom, i-genius was established as a social networking site for social entrepreneurs worldwide.[98] In Australia, an organization called Our Community provides active support to thousands of community-based organizations.[99] Foundations such as Ashoka, Skoll, Omidyar, and Schwab are active in funding ISE pursuits.

International social entrepreneurs are busy transforming the global community. They are carrying out active agendas that address social issues such as poverty, inequality, crime, disease, corruption, the environment, and many others. These individuals play an important role in international civic cooperation in the 21st century.

International social entrepreneurs and like-minded individuals are growing in numbers. A report from the Yearbook of International Organizations reports the existence of over 25,000 citizen-sector organizations, up from a mere 6,000 in 1990.[100] In the United States, there are over 1.4 million nonprofit organizations, and about 26% of U.S. adults claim to have participated in volunteer work.[101] Volunteer hours in the United States alone total about 3 billion.[102] In the United Kingdom, a 2006 report indicated there were about 55,000 social enterprises with a turnover of over 27 billion British pounds.[103] Throughout the world, millions are participating in philanthropic work and community volunteer activities.

Several new and highly innovative social enterprise ventures are emerging. In 2008, *Fast Company* cited the 10 top social enterprise companies. The list included (a) Do Something—an enterprise that aims to increase teen involvement in social development;[104] (b) Mercy Corps—an antipoverty firm focused on helping small-scale lenders by providing them with support and tools and survive and prosper;[105] (c) Academy for Urban Leadership, which provides teacher training programs for often-challenging urban locations;[106] (d) DataDyne, which created and marketed a software that helps public health workers in emerging nations better manage paperwork and data entry;[107] (e) Civic Ventures, which helps address the shortage of managers in the nonprofit sector by recruiting successful baby boomers looking for new careers and engaging them in mentoring and internship programs;[108] (f) Institute for One World Health—a not-for-profit pharmaceutical firm that focuses on key international diseases that need drug development;[109] (g) Acumen Fund—a company that created a data management system designed to help donors and philanthropic investors better manage their resources;[110] (h) Husk Power Systems—a company that developed a technology that allows the conversion of rice husks into biogas for power plants;[111] (i) Hopelab—a company that developed video games designed to help teens deal with and manage ailments;[112] and (j) Enterprise Community Partners—a company focused on providing affordable housing for the poor and for revitalizing communities.[113]

While there is growing interest in social enterprises, active participation by more socially inclined individuals is needed. In the words of Fields Wicker-Miurin, winner of the 2001 Global Leader for Tomorrow Award granted by the World Economic Forum, "Most of the world's problems are too big to be solved by any one leader, they need to be solved together."[114]

Furthermore, greater cross-industry collaborations and organizational alignments are necessary. According to Billy Shore, Chairman of Community Wealth Partners, a consulting firm serving nonprofit organizations, "It is more important than ever that business and nonprofits work together in new ways that bridge market gaps and generate resources necessary to address social needs."[115]

In this book, a seven-step process for the practice of ISE is introduced. The seven-step process is derived from combined research on social entrepreneurship and business internationalization. Several theories, along with anecdotal evidences from stories and cases, are used in generating the recommendations and conclusions outlined in the book.

Step 1: Assess personal and corporate citizenship. Social entrepreneurs should understand their strengths, skills, competencies, and inclinations in order make a meaningful contribution. A thorough self- and corporate assessment is essential. Chapter 2 offers insights on relevant factors that should be considered in assessing personal and corporate citizenship.

Step 2: Understand the environment. A keen understanding of the operational environment where one intends to conduct business is vital. Chapter 3 highlights business and environmental considerations that can contribute to international social enterprise success.

Step 3: Identify an appropriate mission. Social entrepreneurs are often defined by their chosen mission. The identification and execution of the right mission is a framework for success. Chapter 4 discusses the key considerations for successful mission identification.

Step 4: Plan for internationalization. Social entrepreneurs have explored many corners of the world in order to expand their mission. The global landscape offers several challenges and opportunities for individuals, corporations, and countries. Chapter 5 identifies key factors that should be considered in the internationalization process.

Step 5: Pursue strategic action. The selected course of action of an enterprise often determines its fate. Chapter 6 outlines the factors that should be considered as business leaders and their companies take on developmental plans in foreign locations.

Step 6: Adjustment and reinvention. Expansion into foreign locations often leads to the uncovering of unexpected challenges. Even the best-made plans need some refinement or enhancement. Chapter 7 stresses the need to implement strategic changes and recommends viable courses of action.

Step 7: Make a personal and corporate impact. The ultimate goal of this book is to offer students, executives, business and government leaders, consultants, and policy makers useful insights concerning the practice of ISE. Chapter 8 integrates lessons learned in all previous sections of the book and offers suggestions and recommendations to help the reader make a positive international impact on a personal or corporate level.

A featured short story titled "The Tale of the Globalist" is offered in the appendix. The fictional story was designed to showcase some of the strategies mentioned in the book. The intent of the story is to inspire readers to take action and practice ISE in their own unique way.

It is debatable whether the practice of ISE is closer to an art or science. Likewise, it is debatable whether the emerging field is a business practice worthy of study and consideration. The reality, however, is that several of the best business schools in the world have embraced the practice of social entrepreneurship. Another reality is that a growing number of individuals and companies worldwide are practicing social entrepreneurship and are reaping the benefits—both in the context of profit as well as the social impact of the work they do. Even more significant is the reality that, in ways big and small, ISE is transforming the global community.

CHAPTER 2

Assess Personal and Corporate Citizenship

For a community to be whole and healthy, it must be based on people's love and concern for each other.

—Millard Fuller

International social entrepreneur Iqbal Quadir had a successful banking career in New York. After experiencing a computer breakdown in his office, he stumbled on the insight that connectivity leads to productivity. Originally from Bangladesh, Quadir had dreamed about making a technological impact in his home country. He transformed his career by establishing GrameenPhone in conjunction with Norway's telecommunication giant, Telco. GrameenPhone introduced mobile phones to the rural villages of Bangladesh. Quadir's objective was to make telecommunications affordable to the villagers in Bangladesh, who typically had to take a bus to the nearest city to make a phone call. Through the financing efforts of local banks, GrameenPhone made $100 mobile phones available to local residents. The concept allowed enterprising villagers to earn a substantial income while providing affordable communication access to the rest of the community. Over the past few years, GrameenPhone's market value was in the vicinity of $205 million a year, and its net income was in the millions.[1]

Iqbal Quadir is an international social entrepreneur. Operating on a global business terrain, individuals like Quadir successfully transform themselves into social-change makers. His business typifies a social enterprise model that combines both profit and social dimensions. Social enterprises are founded by individuals who blend business acumen and social conscience.[2] The successful practice of international social entrepreneurship (ISE) requires a keen understanding of strengths, inclinations, and capabilities on both personal and corporate levels. Through a well-defined personal and corporate citizenship assessment, international social entrepreneurs gain a heightened understanding of what they are about and what they can do.

Personal Assessment

It is important for international social entrepreneurs to conduct an objective personal assessment and to take into account skills, interests, and goals when planning an international social enterprise. It is equally relevant to consider how personal and organizational goals relate to each other. The following paragraphs outline useful strategies for personal assessment.

Have a clear understanding of one's passion. Since international social entrepreneurs are driven by a desire to make deep, positive impacts, a clear understanding of their passion is essential. This requires the creation of a business model that balances personal goals and enterprise viability. For instance, Parag Shah's vision and mission pertained to helping artists enhance their income. In 2003, Shah founded ArtSwitch.com with the intent of helping artists gain recurring income for their work. The company operates like a club or library where membership fees are collected from members. Members can borrow artwork in exchange for a membership fee of about one British pound a day. In the end, artists get a broad exposure for their work and earn substantially from the leased artwork. Members, on the other hand, get cost savings and gain access to a variety of artwork to display on their premises. The company's model, which combines both social and profit dimensions, redefined the art industry.[3] "Social entrepreneurship is a win–win . . . the entrepreneur gains great personal satisfaction while addressing a social need."[4]

Understand real motives. International social entrepreneurs need to carefully examine their motives and decide what they are about and what they can change. There are several drivers of social entrepreneurship, including need for innovation, support of a mission, provision of income, job creation, and concept licensing.[5] In the words of Molly Barker, founder of Girls on the Run, "When I started the company, my desire was to positively impact lives of young girls . . . we never know the impact of that touch, love, and encouragement on their lives."[6]

Have self-evaluation and goal clarity. Through self-assessment and clear goals, formation of a high-impact social enterprise becomes possible. It is important for social entrepreneurs to examine their core competencies and identify where they can make substantial contributions. Social entrepreneurs tend to form socially oriented ventures in response to an enhanced understanding of themselves and the need to make a difference in the global community.[7] KaBOOM is a social enterprise that builds playgrounds in cities across America. The company's founder, Darrell Hammond, read a newspaper story recounting how two children died of suffocation while playing in an abandoned car. The children opted to play in the car since there were no playgrounds in the area. Hammond was touched by the story and soon embarked on a successful mission of building playgrounds for children.[8]

Exhibit objective assessment and early support. Personal assessment is best backed by reliable information and trustworthy sources. As new ventures are formed, founders initially discuss their ideas with family members to test their ideas, and then rally for support across networks. Information is often gathered in an expeditious manner. Attention is directed toward individuals or organizations that provide resources, commitment, and other forms of support. New contacts are created, and past relationships are revitalized. In its early stages, KaBOOM gained early funding from the Home Depot Foundation. The support provided a stimulus for future growth. In 2005, KaBOOM and Home Depot launched an aggressive $25 million program to build or renovate 1,000 playgrounds in 1,000 days. With media hype and a groundswell of supporters, KaBOOM gained the support of many other companies, such as the Mutual of Omaha Foundation and 24 Hour Fitness.

Exhibit personal and organizational motivation. In the process of self-assessment, understanding personal and organizational motivational factors is important. The process of venture formation consists of three phases: (a) motivation, where the concept is first developed; (b) planning, where preparation is made to initiate the venture; and (c) establishment, where focus is placed on establishing and operating the enterprise.[9] In the case of social enterprises, the motivation phase strongly shapes the course of the venture and its ability to make an impact on the community. As a company, KaBOOM stayed motivated and expanded their concept to attract a larger audience. They built skate parks to reach out to more children. "Motivation is an important component . . . commitment is key and belief in a cause is like belief in a product for a mainstream enterprise—you cannot sell your vision unless you believe in it."[10]

Have core competency and offer value. Social enterprises need to understand their true competencies and the real value they offer. Many social enterprises are centered on the founder's past business success, network, skills, and know-how in a career or business. The entrepreneurs leverage their management and entrepreneurial skills to create a socially directed initiative. Virgin Group founder Richard Branson offered to donate $3 billion of his fortune to further global renewable energy sources. Molly Barker, founder of Girls on the Run, helps preteen girls enhance their self-image and develop healthy lifestyles through running. Her background and experience prepared her for the calling. Molly has a master's degree in social work and participated four times in triathlon competitions in Hawaii.[11]

Exhibit organizational leadership and success. In social enterprises, leadership is essential. Social entrepreneurs are endowed with leadership skills and an innovative spirit that can transform societies.[12] The leadership they provide is behavioral in nature, filters throughout the organization, and sets the framework for the implementation of effective strategies. In the case of KaBOOM, Darell Hammond's leadership was instrumental in the creation of a dynamic and high-impact enterprise.

Consider training and scaling ability. In personal assessment, there is a need to consider training and development, to gain supporters, and to strengthen business models. Social enterprises have a strong human development component that is evident in training programs. The Mill Center at Dixon Hall is a furniture manufacturer and retailer specialized in woodworking and welding. They have a mission to hire the homeless and train them. In order to be sustainable, the company has a dual mission of providing training while generating revenue through the sale of furniture.[13] Social enterprises use training centers as a medium to educate partners and supporters. For instance, KaBOOM created the University of Play (UPlay) and Workshops Entirely on Play (WEPlay)[14] to stimulate interest and generate a common mind-set among its stakeholders. The ability to train and gather support on a large scale was instrumental in the venture's success.

Have an innovative and creative angle. Apart from a passion and clear mission, successful social enterprises have a creative flair and are proactive innovators. Social entrepreneurs are process-doers that act outside of the traditional methodologies of business, governance, and philanthropy, and focus on social reform.[15] In the case of KaBOOM, instead of simply opening up chapters, the company empowered communities to build playgrounds by providing toolkits, training, and other forms of technical assistance. They used the web strategically by making toolkits available online so that interested parties and communities have the resources to raise funds and to organize and develop their own community playgrounds.[16]

Establish business model and fit. In the assessment process, there is a need to establish a fit between personal goals and the selected business model. This means selecting operational approaches that are executable in a timely manner and that are in line with goals and values. In social entrepreneurship, the ability to recognize and seize an opportunity, and then execute sound and moral judgments, is vital.[17] The social enterprise Vision Support Trading has a mission of providing support for the visually impaired. While growing, a steady income stream was required. The management team decided to offer a unique service to corporations that included converting literature to large text, introducing Braille options, and providing for audio recordings. They transformed their business model from one that was focused on charity to one with a stronger business emphasis. Simultaneously, they pursued an aggressive growth agenda that involved identification of grants and supporting government policies, formal business planning to manage risk, collaboration with external experts, and travel to foreign locations to learn about relevant business models.[18] The company grew to be a highly profitable enterprise, utilizing a business model that closely fit the founder's personal and organizational goals.

Explore synergies. In the assessment process, identifying goal and function synergies is essential. While growing a business, it is not uncommon to form new enterprises while simultaneously operating others. This approach has been observed in social enterprises as well. For instance, Sylvan Beach is a social enterprise that provides life skills and employment training for men who have been described as "at risk." In carrying out their social mission, the firm continually evolved and experimented with different business models. In a span of a few years, they created several businesses, such as lawn care, an ice cream parlor, a coffee shop, a catering business, and a café. The company provided program participants the opportunity to engage in these businesses while attending GED and life skills–building classes.[19] The firm actively sought synergies, and a string of enterprises were created to support and expand their mission.

A closer examination of the attributes and mind-set of the social entrepreneur is helpful in understanding the personal characteristics of this type of person. An examination of these characteristics aids in determining whether one fits the social entrepreneur's mold. Gathered research from the literature suggests that attributes of social entrepreneurs are divided into two types: (a) socially focused characteristics and (b) business-focused characteristics.

Socially Focused Characteristics

Socially focused characteristics are attributes of social entrepreneurs that facilitate responses to social issues. These attributes constitute the "heart" of the social entrepreneur and drives them to make an impact on societies. The following attributes are defining characteristics.

Visionaries. Social entrepreneurs have visions that transcend complex situations and issues.[20] Molly Barker of Girls on the Run has been described as a visionary for launching a nationwide running and coaching program for preteen girls. The program attracted thousands of volunteers who serve as role models and coaches for the girls in a 12-week, 24-lesson curricula. The supporters are called SoleMates, and there are two types of programs: Girls on the Run (3rd to 5th graders) and Girls on Track (6th to 8th graders). The success of the program led to the creation of 150 councils throughout the United States and Canada. The program attracted sponsors such as New Balance Athletic Shoes and Apparel Company, Kellogg's Frosted Flakes, and Goody Hair Products.[21] According to Barker, "The ability to see and communicate the big picture and vision of the organization is essential."[22]

Change makers. Social entrepreneurs view the world with a unique perspective and are driven to make a positive impact.[23] They are "catalysts" of change,[24] and they are driven by change and outcomes.[25] Many social entrepreneurs are private citizens focused on a social issue and are driven by innovative ways to address social concerns.[26] They are motivated by the impact of their work rather than by money.[27] They have a sincere motivation to improve communities[28] and to contribute resources and management skills toward community improvement.[29] Through creativity, opportunity identification, and efficient use of resources, they have the ability to make the improbable happen.[30] Robert McEwan founded a social enterprise called Medbank. The company provides free prescription medicines for low-income members of society. McEwan changed the dynamics in which medicines are made available to the needy. Aware that pharmaceutical companies operate Patient Assistance Programs (PAPs), where medicine is provided for free to eligible participants, Medbank chose to facilitate the link between pharmaceutical companies and consumers. The company was invaluable in providing convenience to consumers by eliminating the need to repeatedly complete voluminous paperwork in order to access pharmaceutical agency programs. "Our company streamlines laborious things . . . we strive to make processes easier."[31] Through the efforts of Medbank, over $20 million worth of medicine is received by needy consumers each year. The company received the support of corporate sponsors such as Astra Zeneca, Merck, Novartis, Pfizer, and Blue Cross Blue Shield.[32]

Effective communicators. Social entrepreneurs tend to be good communicators.[33] Excellent oral and written communication skills are extremely important in order to operate a successful social enterprise."[34] Social entrepreneurs are able to clearly convey their message to stakeholders. The simplicity of their message makes the company memorable to the target audience. For instance, TROSA, a social enterprise dedicated toward helping substance abusers, has a very simple motto—"Each one, teach one."[35] Another social enterprise, Kiva.org, is the first person-to-person microlending website. The company clearly conveys its mission in a short phrase—"Connect people through lending to alleviate poverty."[36]

Grounded on ethics and integrity. Social entrepreneurs have a well-placed sense of ethics[37] and an established integrity that lets them gather resources in order to achieve goals.[38] Ten Thousand Villages is a social enterprise that sells "fair price" handicrafts. The company works with over 130 artisan groups in 38 countries. Products they sell include jewelry, home decor, and gifts. The company's business model is based on five fair-trade principles for all artisans: cash advances and prompt final payments, fair price, long-term relationships, design collaboration, and environmental responsibility. The integrity they built and their commitment to better the lives of their partners attracted top-quality and committed suppliers.[39]

Strategic networkers. Social entrepreneurs are creative network developers[40] and team players,[41] and they have the ability to gather commitment and motivate action from stakeholders.[42] "Social entrepreneurs need to be well networked—you need people around you who will bang the drum for you, and help you build a team, access finance, etc."[43] Global Resolve, an endeavor by the Arizona State University dedicated to helping address social issues in Africa, is an excellent example. In carrying out their social mission, they have partnered with schools, local leaders, civic organizations, and foundations to make a meaningful contribution to society.

These possessed attributes point to the highly entrepreneurial nature of the social entrepreneur, as well as a strong desire to pursue social change.

Business-Focused Characteristics

Business-focused characteristics refer to attributes possessed by social entrepreneurs that facilitate enterprise growth and development. These attributes may be described as the "brain" of the social entrepreneur. The following characteristics are defining characteristics.

Goal driven. Social entrepreneurs are goal driven[44] and passionate about achieving their goals.[45] "Tenacity is a crucial attitude for social entrepreneurs."[46] Many goals of social entrepreneurs are formed as a result of the founder's personal or social interests. In the United Kingdom, social entrepreneurship start-ups have been common in recreation, education, and support and care services.[47] These enterprises are aligned with the founder's experience, interests, networks, and personal goals. In the case of KaBOOM, the company constantly expands mission awareness. The firm launched a National Campaign for Play and also created a PlayMaker Network to rally more individuals into action. Moreover, they launched a recognition program called Playful City USA that recognized communities with active and innovative agendas for play activities.[48]

Action oriented. Social entrepreneurs are active solution finders rather than disengaged spectators.[49] YouthBuild has a mission of helping the youth rebuild communities and their lives. Cognizant of the fact that knowledge is important, they started an Academy of Transformation to provide training. In an effort to reach out to their target markets, they introduced Academy to Go, a program that delivers transformation-training modules in various locations.[50] From their actions, it is evident that the company does not watch their business happen—they make it happen.

Innovative and resourceful. Social entrepreneurs are innovative and resourceful.[51] They come up with new methodologies. For instance, a social enterprise called ECT brings recycling closer to the markets that need them.[52] Also in the area of recycling, Green-Works collects old furniture, refurbishes it in an environmentally friendly manner, and then sells it to educational institutions and civic organizations at bargain prices.[53] Committed social entrepreneurs share this innovative spirit. In the words of the CEO of Medbank, Robert McEwan, "What makes our company unique is that we are years ahead of others in using the Internet in our licensed approaches."[54] Innovation helps social enterprises gain a competitive edge and sets the stage for offering real value to target markets.

Financially savvy. Many social entrepreneurs believe that prolonged change is viable only when accompanied by venture earnings.[55] Social entrepreneurs are business oriented[56] and make efficient use of resources.[57] KickStart is a social enterprise that introduces innovative products to the African market. The company has been involved in programs relating to agriculture, shelter, water, sanitation, health, and relief. The company implements a five-step process in their business: (a) identify opportunities, (b) design products, (c) establish a supply chain, (d) develop the markets, and (e) measure and move along. When considering business opportunities, founders Nick Moon and Martin Fisher often ask themselves key questions:

1. What businesses will be profitable in this location?
2. What new tools will be necessary?
3. How can we produce the products?
4. How do we convince someone with limited resources to make a financial commitment?
5. Is this going as planned?
6. What changes are necessary?[58]

KickStart made significant inroads in locations such as Kenya, Tanzania, and Mali. Their website points out impressive statistics: 129,000 products sold; 82,900 enterprises created; 414,000 people taken out of poverty; $83.8 million in new profits and wages generated each year; $300 to get one family out of poverty; and $60 to get one person out of poverty.[59] The financial acumen of social entrepreneurs is evident in their ventures. Some social entrepreneurs with success in one area create new ventures and spin off into other enterprises.[60]

Diversity of backgrounds and endeavors. Social entrepreneurs come from all parts of the world and from all walks of life. Social entrepreneurship seems to attract people from diverse backgrounds, and it is particularly appealing to women. A study pointed out that there is a higher probability for women to engage in social ventures than traditional ventures.[61] In the United Kingdom, one study indicated that social entrepreneurship activities are higher among black and minority ethnic (BAME) groups than among whites.[62] Social entrepreneurs come from many countries, are of different ages and social classes, have diverse education and religion, and pursue initiatives in all types of conceivable industries. In carrying out their work, social entrepreneurs are likely to collaborate with diverse personalities and backgrounds.

International orientation. Social enterprise projects spread their reach internationally. There is an emergence of internationally and civic-oriented actors functioning as noninstitutional bodies that are transforming the global agenda.[63] For instance, David Green founded Project Impact with the intention of making health care products available to the poor across several countries.[64]

The business-focused attributes of social entrepreneurs highlight their keen sense of business and management. In assessing one's suitability to the practice, it is therefore important to consider the knowledge, training, and experience one possesses and how it fits with a planned enterprise.

Personal assessment is a key first step for potential social entrepreneurs. This self-understanding is essential from business conception through the growth of the mission. Pepin, Tranqueda, Baker and Associates, a social enterprise consulting firm, pointed out in a report on social enterprise that social enterprises need to continually stay true to their values and know the primary business purpose.[65] With heightened understanding of one's skills, inclinations, and attitudes, it becomes easier to pursue planned missions and make valuable contributions to society.

Corporate Assessment

Aside from a personal assessment, it is equally important to evaluate the organization and to understand the factors shaping its citizenship in a global environment. Globalization has reshaped the concept of citizenship,[66] as it has broken down social, political, and economic boundaries across countries.[67] Companies worldwide, especially international social enterprises, are well positioned to make a lasting impact. It is essential for private and government organizations to assess their strengths, contributions, and inclinations, and to think through approaches whereby they can bring about positive change.

With global integration, corporations are in the position of being "global corporate citizens."[68] In today's society, companies are measured not only in terms of business strength but also in terms of their level of corporate citizenship.[69] In assessing corporate citizenship, there is value in understanding the factors that define and affect citizenship. Contemporary corporate citizenship is characterized by the features discussed in the following paragraphs.

Driven by value. Ronald Berenbeim, principal researcher for The Conference Board, cited the need for value-based enterprises (VBEs), where companies cater to needs pertaining to financial resources (private capital) as well as goodwill and support of the citizenry (public capital).[70] For instance, nonprofit organizations are in the position of being guardians of values, providing unique services, advocating timely issues, and building social capital.[71] An excellent relevant example would be Transparency International, a company leading the global campaign against bribery and corruption.

Need for proactive participation. The academic literature highlights the need for proactive participation in serving the needs of society. The concept of civil society stresses an element of community life where, in unison, members seek to identify purpose, advocate issues, and build social capital.[72] A resource-based view suggests that organizations need resources, and, therefore, they are required to interact with others to thrive and survive.[73] Another viewpoint, the institution-based view, points out that organizations are part of a society, political arrangement, or industry, and therefore need to coordinate with others.[74] In either case, corporate involvement in issues affecting society is important.

Broader organizational role. Citizenship is associated with measures that create a "civic identity."[75] Corporate citizenship is the degree to which businesses meet economic, legal, ethical, and other responsibilities set by society.[76] It is aligned with the concepts of "social investing"[77] and "social capital."[78] Corporate citizenship initiatives have expanded and have focused on strengthening welfare or improving conditions of sectors that have received little or no attention.[79]

Multisectoral involvement. Organizations engaged in social issues are increasing. In the case of philanthropy, active participation has been evident among entrepreneurs, corporate managers, and financial executives.[80] Inter-organizational alliances and cross-industry collaborations in social programs have grown. In America, corporate citizenship is noticeable not only among social entrepreneurs but also in private corporations. Many companies are actively involved in social causes. Corporations such as Gap, Inc., Apple, Starbucks, Timberland, and American Express participate in social programs. Private corporations have supported social enterprises. In the case of the National Foundation for Teaching Entrepreneurship (NFTE), an enterprise dedicated to building entrepreneurial skills among low-income youth, companies such as MetLife and Pitney Bowes have provided support. Endeavor, an enterprise that supports high-impact entrepreneurs in several countries, has been supported by companies such as Citigroup, the International Finance Corporation, and Salesforce. YouthBuild was supported by organizations such as Bank of America, the Bill & Melinda Gates Foundation, the Ford Foundation, the Charles Stewart Mott Foundation, the Skoll Foundation, the Omidyar Network, Wal-Mart, and the Kellogg Foundation. The World Economic Forum highlighted the need to move beyond just corporate charity and the need for companies to contribute more by integrating global citizenship in their business goals and strategies.[81]

Diverse viewpoints on the role of corporations. There are several viewpoints on the roles that corporations should play in our society. Economist and author Milton Friedman suggests that firms should, first and foremost, follow legal frameworks while earning an income base.[82] Some scholars believe that the role of the corporation is broader and should include legal, economic, ethical, and related responsibilities. Contemporary business thinking suggests that corporations should broaden social horizons and develop international agendas. In January 2002, 34 CEOs from the largest multinational corporations signed a statement of commitment toward global corporate citizenship.[83] Author C. K. Lehman classifies companies into four types: (a) saints—those that uphold legal requirements and have a high impact on the needs of the society; (b) pharisees—those that uphold legal requirements and have a low impact on the needs of society; (c) cynics/repenters—those that violated legal requirements but made a high impact on the goals of the society; and (d) sinners—those that violated legal requirements and made a low impact on the needs of society. Based on this classification, most social enterprises would be characterized as "saints."

Different extent of participation. In social enterprises, the giving philosophy seems to be closely intertwined with missions, goals, and values.[84] Giving offers personal satisfaction and social gratification. Many social enterprises impact societies in deeper ways. Corporate citizenship is classified into four levels: (a) minimalist—with emphasis directed toward the organization and its investors; (b) philanthropic—with emphasis on charitable giving; (c) encompassing—where actions are implemented based on a wide number of stakeholders that interact with the organization; and (d) social activist—where proactive actions are implemented and aimed at making positive changes in the entire society.[85] Based on this classification, social enterprises such as Partners in Health (an emerging nations health care provider) would be categorized as "encompassing" and as a "social activists."

Matching brands with the right social issues. Corporate sponsors carefully assess the fit between their brand or image and the social issue they support. Corporate sponsors and supporters participate in projects that relate to their products. For instance, Philip Morris participated in a program called "Campaign for Tobacco-free Kids." SpecSavers Optical Group supported the UK-based social enterprise Guide Dogs for the Blind. Lenovo, LabCorp, and Cisco supported Kramden Institute, Inc., in their mission to provide computers for disadvantaged students. Business Moves Group (BMG), a moving company, and Steelcase, an office products firm, supported Green-Works, a furniture recycler. Other companies support projects that provide the opportunity to enhance their brand or that are aligned with the social inclinations of the management team. Timberland supported the efforts of an organization called City Year, a firm that implements socially relevant projects in communities across America.

High stakeholder expectations. Contemporary organizations are expected to contribute more to society. Social enterprises aspire to four levels of return for their firms: (a) return on investment, (b) social return on investment, (c) financial return on investment, and (d) emotional return on investment.[86] With several goals and expectations, these companies offer highly innovative products and services and conduct business using creative organizational forms.

International reach. Social enterprises respond to social needs in both the local and international communities. These firms leveraged social contributions in order to gain profitability and corporate value. Green-Works responded to international calls in Sierra Leone, Sudan, and Ghana and successfully shared their expertise. Studies show that firms supporting socially directed initiatives uphold both the best interests of shareholders and the executive team.[87]

Emergence of the social enterprise model. One of the most meaningful approaches for corporate citizenship is the engagement in social entrepreneurship. The number of practitioners has increased in recent years, and many more are inspired to follow. In a survey in the United Kingdom, about 6% of the business population claimed that they were part of a socially directed entrepreneurial endeavor.[88] Considering the total number of businesses in existence, this is a significant proportion of the business community. Companies in diverse industries have joined the social enterprise revolution. Social enterprises such as Grameen Bank, New Source Staffing, Ten Thousand Villages, Ripple Effects, and thousands more are converging their profit and social goals.

Corporate and social enterprise alliance. Large multinational corporations have developed creative linkages and alliances with socially directed organizations. Nicoderm CQ products were endorsed by the American Cancer Society. Coca-Cola did not just donate cash to the Boys & Girls Clubs of America—they entered into a marketing contract with them. Ben & Jerry's, a popular ice cream seller and franchise, launched a program called "PartnerShop," where they engaged in partnerships with community groups without franchise fees and offered full support in facilitating income generation for social programs.

Growing support for social enterprises. Other private corporations and organizations have taken measures to promote the practice of social entrepreneurship. Media organizations and publications, such as the *Wall Street Journal* and *Technology Review*, have recognized entrepreneurial firms with a social purpose. Leading educational institutions understand the appeal of social enterprises and their impact on society. Educational institutions have created research centers focused on enhancing the understanding of social enterprises. For instance, the Social Enterprise Initiative (Harvard University), the Center for Social Innovation (Stanford University), and the Research Initiative on Social Entrepreneurship (Columbia University) are examples of academic institutions that see the relevance of the social enterprise.

Social enterprise as a model for corporate citizenship Social enterprises, as a stand-alone or in partnership with large private corporations and government institutions, are dynamic models for corporate citizenship. Research suggests that markets are wide open for sectors serving the poorer segments of society, including areas such as education, energy, agriculture, finance, and technology, among others.[89]

In examining the factors shaping the contemporary corporate landscape, it is evident that several external factors affect and influence the course of actions of corporations. It is also evident that there is a diversity of actions pursued by companies in regard to global citizenship. Furthermore, while challenges exist, there are unique opportunities for social program collaboration, sponsorship, and the creation of international social enterprises.

In assessing one's organizational readiness to utilize the social enterprise model in order to expand a corporate citizenship agenda, it is important to understand the social enterprise's inherent characteristics. Research studies suggest that social enterprises have two sets of attributes—socially anchored and business anchored—which are described in the following sections.

Socially Anchored Attributes

Socially anchored attributes refer to the organizational attributes of social enterprises that facilitate their responses to social issues.

Focused on impact on society. Social enterprises have a "double bottom line" that combines economic and social benefits.[90] Such enterprises are driven by social responsiveness,[91] and they provide a unique value to society, as do nonprofit organizations that are caretakers of value systems, providers of service, and conquerors of pressing social issues.[92] These entrepreneurial firms have the potential to deal with key social issues, such as poverty,[93] and have been active in dealing with community problems such as drug abuse, environmental conservation and protection, and health and nutrition, among many other issues. NFTE, an enterprise that helps build entrepreneurial skills among young people in low-income communities, has a passionate vision that "every young person will find a pathway to prosperity." This organization operates in 22 states and 12 countries and has trained over 230,000 young people. Their core values include individuality, initiative, and community.[94]

Social enterprises have implemented a diverse set of approaches in addressing social issues. For example, Professor Paul Bloom of Duke University identified the strategies implemented by firms in campaigns against poverty as (a) capital provision, (b) business development assistance, (c) resource matching, (d) provision of niche products and services for the poor, (e) improvement of education, (f) information provision and advocacy, and (g) quality of life enhancement. There are two forms of social services: (a) new program and service providers—those that address issues such as illiteracy and drug addiction in an innovative way, and (b) niche sector providers—those that target specialized groups, such as a specific ethnic group or those with disabilities or specific diseases, among many others.[95] The impact that social enterprises and service organizations have on society can be deep. Nonprofit organizations allow the experimentation of democracy alongside a social conscience.[96] Through the right program, social entrepreneurs can make far-reaching impacts that contribute to dramatic changes in society.[97] Social enterprises can be the means to revive struggling communities, nurture social consciousness, and expand service deliveries in an efficient manner.[98] These types of organizations serve as vehicles through which a healthy civil society may be nurtured.[99] Social enterprises offer economic benefits through implementing business efficiencies and social benefits when the organizations impact communities.[100] Their entrepreneurial focus transforms communities,[101] especially in the area of job creation.[102] This entrepreneurial emphasis sets the foundation for sustainability and deep social changes.[103] Without social enterprises, many communities could not grow to their full potential.[104] Social entrepreneurship is especially helpful in tough economic times or when government funds are constrained.[105] Despite the numerous successes of social enterprises, there is still much to be learned. For instance, there is still a lack of general understanding of the overall impact social enterprises provide.[106]

Pursuit of change. Social enterprises are facilitators of change.[107] The goal of social change is driven by passion and a need to act in order to pursue change.[108] Heifer International is a social enterprise that is pushing to make dramatic changes. This organization is focused on building sustainable communities that fight world hunger and poverty and that care for the environment at the same time. The company teaches environmentally sensitive agricultural practices in several countries.

Clear vision. Social enterprises have a clear understanding of their mission. Studies suggest that organizations that crystallize their concept and communicate effectively in the mind-set of their target audience create a significant impact.[109] Habitat for Humanity is an example of an enterprise with a clear and understandable mission. Nike's global thinking is evident in their vision statement, "Our vision is to be an innovative and inspirational global citizen in a world where our company participates."[110] KaBOOM's vision explicitly describes the company's agenda: "Our vision is a great place to play within walking distance of every child in America."[111]

Policy changers and transformers. Market forces drive social change.[112] Social entrepreneurship is a way to limit reliance on grants, donations, and subsidies.[113] It seals gaps in funding that are not adequately provided by different levels of government.[114] Social entrepreneurship provides a platform for governments to focus on other needs.[115] For instance, the social enterprise Partners in Health (PIH), when dealing with illnesses in emerging locations, pressures drug manufacturers, provides medical care, and lobbies to policy makers to solve medical problems.[116] In 2006, the social enterprise Endeavor (Mexico division) lobbied to major political parties to integrate high-impact entrepreneurship in their campaign agendas. The campaign led to favorable changes and results.

Commitment to stakeholders. Social enterprises have a high sense of accountability toward stakeholders.[117] Studies suggest that strong connection with stakeholders is essential for venture sustainability.[118] According to social entrepreneur Liam Black (CEO of Fifteen), attention has to be paid to excluded groups.[119] In nonprofit organizations, investing in resources to project the right image[120] and balancing the demands of various stakeholders[121] are two essential components of operation.

Anchored on credibility. Social enterprises need to demonstrate they are legitimate and credible enterprises.[122] Sheetal Mehta, an executive of the social enterprise Shivia, indicated that social claims have to be real and credible.[123] Social entrepreneur Liam Black underscored the need for efficient social reporting.[124] The KickStart organization highlights the importance of trust building and product awareness.[125] The company has successfully launched products, helped communities, and created a well-recognized brand in Africa.

Business-Anchored Attributes

Business-anchored attributes refer to social enterprise organizational attributes that facilitate responses to business opportunities.

Market oriented. Nonprofit organizations have high propensity toward market orientation.[126] This keen market awareness facilitates the identification of meaningful opportunities. Brooklyn Justice Counsel is a socially directed enterprise that offers low-cost legal services to members. The company conducted focus groups to better understand consumer mindsets and to identify suitable services. The results of their research helped them define a successful growth strategy.[127] KickStart cites a need for sales and marketing approaches suited to market conditions.[128] Social enterprise consulting firm Pepin, Tranqueda, Baker and Associates underscores the need to clearly define target market, competitors, competition mode, pricing differentiation, quality and competitive advantages, competitor's strengths and weaknesses, and the barriers to entry and exit.[129]

Double bottom line. While social enterprises are socially anchored, they have to earn continuous income in order to be sustainable. They are pursuing a "double bottom line," and they strive for social gains alongside financial betterment.[130] In the case of Ten Thousand Villages, while helping artisans is an important component of their mission, the company is aware that their ability to sell the products and stay profitable is critical for venture sustainability. The nonprofit organization Food Share Toronto provides education and access to affordable and healthy food. In striving for program sustainability, this organization focuses on reduction of overhead costs, operational efficiencies, and building on program synergies in order to optimize returns.

Entrepreneurial mind-set. Social enterprises need an entrepreneurial framework to be sustainable and to pursue desired social changes.[131] For instance, an entrepreneurial attribute such as resourcefulness is essential. In striving to raise funds, Guide Dogs for the Blind Association encouraged supporters to donate disregarded and broken watches, jewelry, and similar accessories. They recycled these items to raise funds for the organization. Another social enterprise, Teacher Support Network, which provides support for the resource needs of educators, created a profit subsidiary to form a structure that differentiates their charity work and business goals. The business division focused solely on profit generation and subsequently facilitated the organization's overall expansion and growth.

Profit oriented. Financial strength is important to a social enterprise. Through social entrepreneurship, a broader access to financial resources may be gained.[132] Financial surplus can be reinvested to further develop the venture. A social enterprise's drive toward securing more income can change the dynamics and direction of an organization.[133] In some cases, income generated from a specific segment or market is used to subsidize a poorer performing one. The KickStart organization highlighted the need for a profitable business model that allows for prompt investment recovery.[134] Greyston Bakery's guiding principles state, "The bakery should consistently achieve operating profit."[135] World of Good underscores the need to continually "monitor progress towards financial goals."[136]

High creativity. Many social enterprises leverage their competencies and abilities in a creative manner.[137] Endeavor supports high-impact entrepreneurs in developing nations. The company's strength lies in people development and capital access. In pursuing its mission, the company showcases role models, provides mentoring and advice, and utilizes its network to attract investment. Endeavor believes that successful entrepreneurs eventually contribute to society by creating jobs, wealth, research opportunities, and innovation. Their ultimate goal is to create societies with robust cultural, financial, human, intellectual, and social capital.[138]

Propensity for innovation. Social entrepreneurship involves innovation.[139] To gather more computers for needy students, Kramden Institute, Inc., launched "Geek-a-thons," where tech-savvy volunteers work together to refurbish as many computers as they can. This innovative approach attracted over 1,000 volunteers who refurbished more than 4,000 computers.[140]

Alliance formers. In today's society, boundaries between market, nonprofit, and government sectors are blurred. Social enterprises operate in a collaborative spirit where everyone's help is welcome.[141] Through their strong social appeal, nonprofit organizations are typically in a unique position to generate trust and support.[142] Social enterprises need to engage in interorganizational partnerships and alliances to be successful.[143] YouthBuild built strong allies in both the public and private sectors. Among the company's supporters and strategic partners are the U.S. Department of Housing and Urban Development, the U.S. Department of Health and Human Services, the U.S. Department of Agriculture, the U.S. Department of the Treasury, Bank of America, Wal-Mart, the Bill & Melinda Gates Foundation, and the Ford Foundation. "Social entrepreneurs need the ability to lead collaboratively engaging all constituents in the process of strategic and big picture thinking."[144]

Sound managers. Social enterprises use sound economic management and business skills when developing their businesses. This requires a well-balanced approach that takes culture, process, and structure into consideration.[145] Author Pamela Hartigan observed the use of the following strategies among social enterprises: (a) leveraging of resources and utilization of surplus, (b) strategic use of technology, (c) proper research, (d) financial analysis, (e) efficient manufacturing and distribution, and (f) attractive and flexible pricing.[146] KickStart's business model emphasizes supply-chain efficiencies, economies of scale, product quality and distribution, as well as market accessibility. The organization seeks to optimize profitability with the resources invested. When developing a new business, the KickStart organization selects products that balance quality, cultural suitability, and sustainability. Research and cases point to the use of sound management practices by social enterprises.

Action oriented. Social enterprises are highly proactive. Social entrepreneurs need to position their social issues as urgent—that is, those needing radical and immediate action.[147] On its website, the social enterprise Teach for America states that it is "working with a great sense of urgency to build a movement to eliminate educational inequity."[148]

Organized for action. In order to achieve their goals, social enterprises should be well organized. Author Pamela Hartigan observed three models of social enterprises: (a) leveraged nonprofit—where an organization is established to promote an innovation; (b) hybrid not-for-profit—where a firm builds on cost efficiencies through sales of products or services, creative partnering, or niche marketing; and (c) hybrid for profit—where a company develops a business to institute a major change that impacts a large number of people and transforms business modalities.[149] The mentioned organizational forms point to an active agenda anchored on innovation and change. Creative organizational forms are often used. In the case of Girls on the Run, 150 councils were formed in the United States and Canada to carry out its mission.

Deal with diversity. Complex issues and problems require dealing with diverse groups of individuals and organizations in order to achieve desired goals and objectives.[150] In pursuing their missions in foreign locations, social enterprises work through diverse cultures, infrastructures, and business modes. In addition, the multifaceted goals they aspire to adds to business complexity. For instance, in their quest to deal with health challenges in emerging nations, PIH implements a multitiered agenda that includes caring for patients, treating causes of disease in their locations, and sharing lessons learned with others around the world. Furthermore, the company deals with diverse issues such as HIV/AIDS, tuberculosis, women's health, child health, food, water, housing, and community health workers. They are simultaneously active in numerous locations, including Haiti, Lesotho, Malawi, Peru, Russia, Rwanda, the United States, Mexico, and Guatemala.[151] Navigating through such complexity on a regular basis forces these enterprises to be inventive, proactive, resourceful, and action oriented.

Conclusion

In examining the organizational attributes of social enterprises, it is evident that these firms draw upon strong social and business foundations in order to be successful. There are several entrepreneurial attributes necessary for social enterprises to flourish. Organizational competencies such entrepreneurial mind-set, creativity, and innovation have to be cultivated and nurtured. Some organizational attributes—such as the socially anchored attribute of vision clarity and the business-anchored attribute of market orientation—need to be present in the early stage of business formation. Other firm attributes—such as the socially anchored attribute of policy changers and transformers and the business-anchored attribute of alliance formers—can be emphasized in an organization's growth stage. In essence, as there are several inherent characteristics that could impact the social enterprise's success, it makes sense for managers to set priorities.

It is a good idea to plot out an organizational growth plan that allows for the nurturing of important attributes in the company's culture.

Similar to personal assessments, organizational assessments should be structured to determine the current level of corporate citizenship and to evaluate the existing mix of attributes that would allow it to operate as a successful social enterprise.

As individuals and corporations exercise their roles as global citizens, a careful assessment of personal and corporate strengths and weaknesses can lead to the identification of precise areas where a valuable contribution to society can be made.

CHAPTER 3

Understand the Environment

Man is not the creature of circumstances; circumstances are the creatures of men.

—Benjamin Disraeli

International social entrepreneur Ted Halstead founded a nonprofit public policy company, Redefining Progress, at the age of 25. By the age of 32, he created two think tanks. Halstead's company is a medium through which new approaches to economic and environmental policy are identified and prominently positioned for discussion in the public arena. At the age of 30, Halstead also established the New America Foundation, which engages a venture capital approach to channel investment in individuals and policy ideas that go beyond the conventional political spectrum. Halstead was instrumental in generating the largest public statement in the history of the economics profession by securing the signatures of more than 2,500 economists in a statement addressing the issue that global warming, via market-based policies, would bolster, rather than damage, a nation's economy.[1]

In this case, Halstead clearly understood the international operating environment. After gaining a thorough understanding of the landscape, he implemented measures to pursue his desired goals. His chosen courses of action had a global impact.

It is important to understand the international operating environment well and to plan accordingly. As a result of globalization, it has become easier to make inroads internationally and gain access to new markets.[2] Consequently, with this ease of access and new technologies, products or services experience shorter marketing time, heightened competition, and condensed life cycles. In the corporate world, many executives create their business development agenda following the framework of a highly interconnected and borderless global society. Though some of these ventures have few employees, they have taken on an international perspective since their formation.

The need to understand operational environments, especially in foreign locations, is not a new concept. Throughout history, military forces in different countries have conducted physical surveys and comprehensive research prior to sending troops to battle. A similar approach is currently being used by global strategists in large multinational corporations. Prior to committing investments in foreign locations, they invest in time, financial resources, and effort directed at understanding the operational terrain well. This is a view shared by social enterprises: "There is a need to understand the systems in place . . . as an outsider (foreign entrant) we can't possibly know all the specifics of navigating cultures and legal systems successfully."[3]

International social entrepreneurs have a keen sense of the market.[4] Global Resolve, an endeavor founded by Arizona State University, facilitates the creation of environment-friendly cooking oil in Ghana that provides for the specific needs of villagers and an income opportunity for a network of people who facilitate product sales.[5] The organization customizes their social endeavors to respond to specific community needs. For instance, an ethanol project in Domeabra, Ghana, focused on serving fuel needs, while in Fawomanye, a water purification project was directed at improving the water supply.

Many nongovernmental development organizations are responding to global forces that homogenize contemporary society. For instance, a concept employed in one country is adaptable in other locations. Ideas gained from one emerging nation can be shared and transferred to similar locations.

Many socially oriented firms are exploring foreign markets in their quest for broadening solutions for social causes, replicating domestic successes, and expanding their reach. This process of internationalization may be viewed as an outward expansion of a firm's endeavor into foreign locations.[6] For example, Ten Thousand Villages has over 100 retail stores that sell "fair price" handicrafts that they have gathered from artisans in emerging nations.

Within the international landscape, many enterprises abruptly carry out expansions.[7] These expansion efforts may leave them empty-handed unless prior research is initiated and there is an understanding of the environment: "Research is essential in international expansion."[8]

Through a sound understanding of the complex business dynamics of an international location, firms are in a better position to anticipate potential problems and capitalize on opportunities. Research suggests that social entrepreneurs need to be aware of their operational environment and frameworks,[9] and they need to heighten sensitivity to the local requirements of new locations.[10] The KickStart organization underscores the importance of cultural suitability of products in foreign venues: "Cultural awareness is an important consideration in internationalization."[11]

Social entrepreneurs have to be aware that operational differences exist in uncharted territories. Though similar features exist across countries, such as the common need to form social networks,[12] the attributes of different countries are unique and require consideration and attention: "Different regulations and legislation govern organizations."[13]

Social enterprises must consider advanced planning and risk assessment. Many internationalizing enterprises have shown lackluster performance in foreign environments as a result of poor planning, haphazard program implementation, and unsubstantiated attitudes toward risk and uncertainty.[14]

Social enterprises need to methodically gather information and need to be prepared to shift strategies. Several studies suggest that internationalizing firms should acquire relevant knowledge through exploration, should challenge assumptions, and should consider new ways of learning.[15] In addition, it is sensible for socially directed organizations to gain knowledge and be proficient in socioeconomic analysis and to seek business solutions that extend beyond the confines of one location.[16]

A keen understanding of the operational environment can lead to distinct advantages, as illustrated in the case of the Bangladesh Rural Advancement Committee. Upon gaining awareness of the market conditions in the country, and through observing a misalignment in the marketing and distribution of some food products, the organization established a cold storage for potatoes. This approach subsequently led to significant revenue generation for the organization, while simultaneously providing countless benefits to producers. Though this case refers to an enterprise operation in a single country, it demonstrates the fact that in emerging markets, market understanding is vital for venture success.

Aside from understanding the operational environment, a firm's ability to build successful networks is critical. In foreign locations, the firm's ability to leverage networks affects its propensity to acquire knowledge[17] and shapes the depth and breadth of the impact it makes.[18] Kiva collaborated with field partners in emerging nations to help promote their mission of finding capital for the poor. Global Resolve linked with different types of entities—schools, civic organizations, and foundations—to successfully implement their projects.

Social enterprises have to respond to transformations of an evolving marketplace, as it is likely that changes will occur in the types of needs, competitive terrain, and availability of resources.[19]

In new environments, social enterprises are likely to face new challenges and opportunities. For instance, in the course of internationalization, firms are influenced by several complex factors. This section explores potential challenges and opportunities that confront social enterprises as they venture into new locations.

Challenges

In developing businesses in foreign locations, firms confront new challenges. These challenges are evident in factors that are *internal* (within the organization) or *external* (outside the organization).

Internal Challenges

Internal challenges refer to factors within an enterprise that are stumbling blocks in new operational environments or in the enterprise's internationalization efforts.

Firm attributes. The way that a firm perceives opportunities, as well as its past activities, impacts its internationalization.[20] The rates of internationalization differ across firms and industries. A popular internationalization theory known as the Uppsala Model, first developed by researchers at the University of Uppsala in Sweden, suggests that firms pursue internationalization slowly and after confidence in their capabilities is gained.[21] This appears to be the case in most social enterprises: "We have expansion requests from over 40 countries, but have put our internationalization on hold until we are satisfied with the systems we use to grow and sustain the organization domestically."[22] The premise is that international expansion takes place across countries gradually, starting with locations where the sociocultural framework is most similar to the home country. The path toward international expansion typically involves steps such as exports, use of agents, sales subsidiaries, production, and marketing subsidiaries.[23]

Management factors. Factors such as availability of management,[24] the management's experiences,[25] and its ability to deal with complexity[26] impact a firm's ability to internationalize. Research suggests that foreign direct investment is limited by factors such as skills availability, organizational capacity, politics, and growth transitions.[27] Diversity of viewpoints regarding what markets to enter, how to enter them, and resource distribution lead to conflicts, misunderstandings, and high communication costs:[28] "It takes several people to manage and operate a social enterprise . . . the skills required come from both the left and right brained folks of the world."[29]

Process-related challenges. Activities pertaining to carrying out an internationalization effort can cause problems. Distraction from the core mission is possible. While internationalizing, firms typically need good partners, [30] clear credibility,[31] and a well-defined plan, along with administrative procedures.[32] Furthermore, internationalization may involve misunderstanding of consumer preferences, government laws and policies, competitive activity, and country infrastructure, which may result in problems:[33] "Cultural awareness, sensitivity, and knowledge are important in internationalization."[34]

Organization and structure. The way that firms structure themselves as they internationalize impacts their ability to succeed. Size poses a challenge for internationalizing firms.[35] Small firms face significant challenges when internationalizing,[36] as they are often unable to pursue suitable opportunities.[37] Research suggests that key challenges in small enterprise internationalization include (a) limited market power, (b) serving only a small segment of a market, and (c) difficulty in the leadership infrastructure responding to challenges.[38] With regard to organizational structure, further research suggests there are relevant merits in the overseas selection of agents and partners[39] and the efficient flow of knowledge and information within the organization.[40] Partners in Health (PIH), a social enterprise with operations in several countries, believes that community partnership is vital to their strategy. Greyston Bakery emphasizes employee empowerment in their business model.

Relationship and linkages. The manner in which an organization cultivates international relationships is important. Research suggests that many international alliances have ended up in failure.[41] Those that have succeeded developed strong local alliances[42] and business networks.[43] As social enterprise YouthBuild expanded into Africa, they partnered with a local youth fund, government agencies, foundations, civic groups, and educational institutions.

Finance related. There are many cost considerations in the internationalization process. Some of these costs are attributable to market imperfections. Firms may simply lack resources,[44] local market conditions may not lead to adequate financial return,[45] and related costs are high.[46] In the case of social enterprises, financial commitment is essential: "Like a normal business, social entrepreneurs need to invest their own resources."[47] International expansion further increases costs such as business transactions, information processes, and communication-related expenses.[48] In some cases, profit reduction may be attributable to learning curves.[49] As firms engage in new operational arrangements overseas, significant resource commitment is necessary.[50] For instance, when a company switches strategies or modes of operations, there are costs associated with the changes, such as "take-down" switching costs.[51] Strategy changes can also result in "set-up" switching costs.[52] Financial mismanagement by managers compound these challenges.

Ability to deal with risk. Due to the political risk in foreign environments, internationalizing ventures are subject to a diverse business hazards. There are threats associated with the internationalization process,[53] and internationalization heightens the risk of failure:[54] "Social problems are hard to solve . . . there are a lot of free riders out there who will take advantage of anyone who is seen to want to do good."[55]

Ethical framework. Ethical conduct of managers impacts the internationalization process and its success. Research studies point out the adverse effect of unethical or self-serving managers.[56] Social enterprises have to be cautious in their selection of collaborators and partners in foreign locations. Several news accounts indicate cases of bribery, corruption, and mismanagement of aid and donations in foreign countries.

Knowledge acquisition. The way that a firm acquires, processes, and utilizes knowledge and information in foreign locations is essential to its success. There are challenges involved in the acquisition of pertinent information and in integrating this information into workable strategies. Studies suggest that the more knowledge a firm has about a location, the greater the resource commitment.[57] In the case of Endeavor, the knowledge they gained from their initial international locations provided a useful knowledge base for other markets.

Communication. Effective communication enhances the internationalization process. Language is a key consideration. Language factors into how information is gathered, processed, and exchanged:[58] "When internationalizing a social enterprise, the ability to speak the language is essential."[59]

Planning ability. Careful planning in foreign ventures is important. Unplanned ventures into foreign locations will lead to failure.[60] Successful social enterprises require careful planning based on research and the creation of a thorough business plan.[61] In some instances, extensive international diversification can lead to performance decline.[62] A new firm that is simultaneously entering domestic and foreign markets needs to create dual sets of solutions and images, and needs to build credibility in both the domestic and foreign locations.[63]

External Challenges

External challenges are factors that exist outside of an enterprise's organization that affect the firm as it ventures into a new location and that affect the firm during the course of its internationalization efforts.

Cultural level. Culture is a factor in entrepreneurial differences across countries.[64] Lack of market familiarity and cultural factors impede internationalization.[65] A report on international social franchising cited that lack of consideration for culture and lack of research were among the reasons for overseas franchising failure.[66] In a similar manner, language factors into how information is gathered, processed, and exchanged.[67] "Social enterprises need cultural awareness, sensitivity, and knowledge to thrive in international environments."[68]

Social level. Several social factors should be considered when expanding overseas. Selection of the wrong partner or having a poor relationship structure contributes to international failure.[69] Companies should seek out good partners,[70] strategic allies,[71] trustworthy agents,[72] and proper business networks.[73] PIH utilized community partnership as part of their successful developmental strategy: "When internationalizing, we need to engage the right people in new locations to deliver our program."[74]

Political factors. There are numerous risks associated with internationalization. In foreign locations, financial and political barriers exist.[75] Currency exchange issues are also potential challenges.[76] Key obstacles in the outward investment of firms include political risks and instability of the economic environment.[77] Social enterprises need to navigate through these types of challenges. For instance, in Mexico, Endeavor had to lobby political parties in order to further their social agenda in the country.

Business and economic factors. Due to the differences between the home and host country environments, certain implemented strategies may be ineffective. Research suggests that internationalization may result in a misunderstanding of consumer preferences, government laws and policies, competitive activity, and country infrastructure, which may all lead to problems.[78] Ten Thousand Villages noted that the artisans they work with are constrained with regard to geography, transportation, and social and organizational factors. In some cases, the competitive landscape is intense,[79] and bureaucracy and operational inefficiencies can result in stumbling blocks.[80] Domestic success causes firms to focus on local opportunities rather than overseas expansion.[81] In their campaign to improve the lives of girls and women in poverty, World of Good believes that navigating through issues such as communication challenges, lack of transportation, lack of efficient supply chains, poor production processes, and diverse industry approaches is critical.[82]

Financial landscape. Financial barriers exist, and these tend to be a result of market imperfections.[83] For instance, in Mexico, Endeavor faced a business landscape where entrepreneurs found it difficult to obtain loans. Similarly, when Endeavor made a market entry in Uruguay, there was no formal venture capital association. The company played a role in eventually creating one.

Legal aspects. In some foreign locations, laws may be ambiguous. Poor consideration of legal aspects is another potential cause for failure in the internationalization process:[84] "As social enterprises internationalize, regulations and legislations should be considered."[85] Bureaucracy and operational inefficiency negatively impact success in foreign shores.[86] "Legal issues pertaining to copyright, trademark, and business structures are important."[87]

From these challenges, it is evident that social enterprises need to respond to obstacles both internally and externally. Internal challenges can be addressed by implementing specific management actions, while external factors are more challenging as they are not entirely within the firm's control. The course of action a firm takes to respond to external challenges determines their success in foreign environments. Social enterprises should, therefore, assess and understand the operational environment and evaluate the environment alongside their organizational attributes. With numerous challenges, identifying critical areas of organizational weakness and correcting them should lead to heightened firm performance. In a similar manner, a firm can also pick out its strong points and build a success strategy from there.

Despite obstacles in the internationalization process, there remain numerous opportunities for developing and expanding into international markets. In the United States, with over 3,500 franchisers in existence, less than 100 are run by nonprofit firms.[88] This suggests there is a lot of room for nonprofit firms to internationalize in the future. Studies suggest that factors such as firm size[89] and age [90] do not necessarily inhibit internationalization. The World Outlook on Franchising cited several countries as having excellent potential for franchising including South Africa, China, Germany, Brazil, Australia, and the United States.[91] With its strong social orientation, international social enterprises can make an impact in several emerging nations around the world.

There are several advantages to be gained by social enterprises as they internationalize. The factors that follow are perceived as opportunities relating to the process of firm internationalization.

Growth. Foreign markets offer growth opportunities and set the stage for firms to pursue it.[92] When internationalizing, new opportunities are explored, and there is less reliance on local markets.[93] International growth should be thought out in a strategic context.[94] For instance, World of Good found they could efficiently replicate their model in international markets such as India, Thailand, Cambodia, Guatemala, Peru, Ghana, Kenya, and South Africa.

Profit. Foreign markets[95] and the internationalization process[96] offer profit opportunities. Internationalization expands profit,[97] leads to income stability,[98] and heightens the chances of a firm's survival.[99] Internationalization also allows for the diversification of revenue sources.[100]

Research suggests that internationalization efforts can lead to a firm's enhanced financial condition and can bring forth strength in leverage.[101] Through KickStart's efforts in Kenya, Tanzania, and Mali, more than 129,000 pieces of their products were sold, and over $83.8 million in new profits and wages were generated each year.[102]

Cost efficiencies. Foreign locations offer cost advantages.[103] For instance, internationalizing firms have the opportunity to take advantage of lower labor costs and lower priced resources. With proper resource utilization, social enterprises can expedite expansion on foreign shores. In just a few years, Healthstore Foundation was able to open and operate 65 child and family wellness (CFW) shops in Kenya.

Competitive advantage. When strategically implemented, internationalization can be a path toward building a competitive advantage.[104] Internationalization can also help build export competencies. In the case of Endeavor, the aggregated knowledge of entrepreneurial modalities in emerging markets they gained helped them become a thought leader and value contributor.

New markets. Internationalization opens the doors to new market opportunities.[105] As Endeavor started supporting entrepreneurs in emerging markets, they started to slowly expand to similar locations. Endeavor started in the United States in 1997. In 1998, they expanded to Argentina and Chile. In 2000 through 2004, they expanded to Brazil, Mexico, and South Africa. From 2005 onward, they expanded to locations such as Turkey, Colombia, Egypt, and India. As the company gained success in emerging nations, similar countries were attracted to their services.

Dealing with competition. Expansion overseas allows some firms to preempt their rivals.[106] This is common in the corporate world, especially in industries that are highly competitive. Licensing and franchising lets firms get ahead of their rivals in foreign locations. Advantages ascribed to both approaches include lower start-up costs, optimization of competitive advantages, revenue opportunities, lowered risk, rapid expansion, learning from new markets, and market expansion.[107] Franchising of social franchises has gained industry interest. Ventures typically franchise in four ways: (a) traditional master license—where an individual or group is a selected franchisee in a geographical area; (b) area developer—where a middleman is selected to sell the franchise in a region; (c) joint venture—where the franchiser contributes capital but acts as a passive investor; and (d) public–private model—where a franchiser provides the franchise license to the government or state-owned enterprise.[108] The National Foundation for Teaching Entrepreneurship, a social enterprise, licenses its programs to nonprofit organizations, schools, and government entities. For selected licensees, the company provides training, project planning assistance, media and marketing support, and limited use of the company's trademark and logo, among other benefits. The company has made successful progress internationally.

Performance efficiencies. Internationalization leads to the improvement of firm performance[109] and also helps in building a global brand.[110] Research studies point out the operational benefits of internationalization, such as international learning,[111] leveraging of strength,[112] and business optimization from fragmented markets.[113] For instance, as PIH carries out its mission of fighting health challenges in emerging nations, experiences learned in one country enhanced their competitiveness in dealing with similar diseases in other locations.

Knowledge and technology gain. Studies suggest that there are knowledge and technological gains to be accrued in the course of internationalization.[114] Endeavor creates cases based on the entrepreneurs they have supported and worked with. These cases are shared with others inside and outside the organization, including in academe. Knowledge learned is therefore shared, and many learn from it.

Conclusion

The list of opportunities indicates that with a clear market understanding and appropriate action agenda, social enterprises have a lot to gain in foreign locations. Since there are several factors that need to be considered, an investment of time, effort, and resources in understanding the foreign location can result in significant future payoffs. A keen understanding of how the opportunities can be effectively pursued, based on existing organizational attributes, is important.

In the process of learning and adapting to a global environment, it is important to understand the attributes of this environment. The social enterprise KickStart, through its keen understanding of the African region, was able to successfully expand and enhance agriculture practices in several countries. Though the global landscape may be depicted in many ways, nine defining attributes are evident, as described in the following paragraphs. Sensitivity and awareness of the implications of each attribute would be helpful to the internationalizing social enterprise.

G—Geographical compression. Breakthroughs in technology, trade integration, and modes of travel have brought the various areas of the world closer together. Activities have become closely linked and tightly enmeshed. Social enterprises can build advantages from this geographic compression. For instance, outsourcing can be utilized as an option to lower costs. This heightened integration also facilitates replication of viable business models in other countries.

L—Liberalization of values. Monoculturalism is a mindset of the past. The rapid and continuous flow of news events, information, and the cross-border flow of cultural products all have led to the homogenization of value systems. As a result, by building on common values and recognizable social needs, international social entrepreneurs can successfully launch their programs in many countries. As an example, social enterprises that cater to popular global causes such as poverty, health, and the environment would likely gain support in many countries.

O—Opportunity for leadership. The stage is set for global leadership. Individuals willing to bring forth change have the opportunity to make far-reaching impacts through the creation of international social enterprises. The world is an international social entrepreneur's paradise.

B—Best is best. The global society has been described as one where the "winners take all."[115] There is constant pressure to excel and be the best. Social enterprises need to implement cutting-edge measures to make their mark and have a profound global impact.

A—Adaptation obsession. Organizations worldwide are adapting to an ever-changing global world. Social enterprises need to have a portfolio of innovative platforms to use and implement. Measures such as organizational transformation, outsourcing, virtualization, e-commerce, social networking, and strategic alliances are essential.

L—Local and global. Individuals and organizations worldwide are experiencing the push and pull forces of globalization. Social enterprise models that tap into local knowledge to build global competitive advantages are gaining popularity. The common thinking is not to pursue either a local or global strategy, but rather to use both approaches in a complementary manner. Social enterprises can be local and global.

I—International knowledge. More than ever, there is a growing need to better understand the international landscape. It is critical to learn about foreign cultures, history, languages, and business and economic environments. Knowledge gained internationally becomes a framework for heightened competencies and paves the way for future success.

Z—Zero in on competitive advantages. Social enterprises need not excel at everything; however, excellence in at least one business attribute is achievable. There is a need to identify and build on at least one key competency to be successful. Furthermore, international social entrepreneurs should hone their skills and should be continually prepared to reinvent themselves and their organization in order to gain a competitive edge.

E—Empowerment. The global environment has strengthened the capabilities of both individuals and organizations. As a result of innovative technologies and heightened integration of nations, international social entrepreneurs are empowered to shape events beyond the boundaries of their home countries and communities. They have gained the ability to touch the lives of others internationally and globally. Globalization has superempowered individuals and corporations.

The global world is complex and challenging. Millions are perplexed by the challenges brought about by globalization; many are struggling to survive. Through a keen understanding of the operational environment, as well as the dynamics of the global arena, international social entrepreneurs can avoid potential pitfalls and plan effective methodologies for success. Understanding the environment means being open to new information and processes, getting ready to quickly accept changes, and preparing to

GLOBALIZE.

CHAPTER 4

Identify the Appropriate Mission

Its not what you think of the "World" that makes a "world" of difference but what the "World" thinks of you.

—John P. Martino

Fields Wicker-Miurin has awakened the world, at least some of it. She helped establish the Wake up, Europe task force. The group created the European Future Readiness Index, which evaluates countries in four broad categories: sustainability, balance between environment and economy, fairness and individual fulfillment, and harmony and readiness for the future. Additionally, she contributes to another task force, Triple Bottom Line, which evaluates the impact business leaders have on people, planet, and profits.[1]

After an organization thoroughly understands itself, the organization's inclinations, and the operating environment, pursuing an appropriate mission becomes a natural next step. Fields Wicker-Miurin found her mission by applying her interests and talents into existing business opportunities while contributing to efficient global governance. She is also an international social entrepreneur.

The success of an international social entrepreneurship initiative relies on the creation and implementation of one's vision and mission. The concept needs to be well developed, and the goals that are set should be achievable.[2]

After assessing personal and corporate citizenship and understanding the operational environment, international social entrepreneurs are in a position to identify a viable and workable mission.

Social entrepreneurs are excellent vision and mission finders and competent in the execution of the mission. The ability to identify a predefined mission is a core element in social entrepreneurship.[3] Marc Freedman, president of Civic Ventures, learned that the nonprofit sector has a large shortage of managers. By 2016, the shortage is estimated to exceed 600,000. He decided to help the sector by recruiting baby boomers looking for "encore" careers. In the process, he ended up providing a successful dual service—jobs for the baby boomers and competent managers for the nonprofit sector.[4]

Social entrepreneurs are visionaries with a high motivation for change.[5] Mark Dribner started a social enterprise called the Kramden Institute to provide computers for needy children. With a clear vision and strong intent to change, he was able to secure cooperation from thousands of supporters and corporate donors. The company organizes "geek-a-thons," where tech-savvy volunteers make a concerted effort to rebuild computers and give them to those who cannot afford to acquire them.[6]

The social entrepreneur's vision has to be anchored in entrepreneurial thinking and venture sustainability. Some researchers underscore the relevance of vision formulation, leadership ability, and long-term impact in the success of a social enterprise,[7] while others highlight the importance of entrepreneurial thinking and action, concretization of goals and aspirations, and venture continuity.[8] Sheetal Mehta, founder of a social enterprise called Shivia, a microfinance facilitator in India and Nepal, expressed the need to pursue vision and goals in the context of profitability.[9]

The social entrepreneur's vision and mission is intertwined with a personal passion. The social entrepreneur's attempt to address social issues is a result of a combination of personal factors, such as spiritual response, personal compassion, belief and ideology, and outrage toward a social issue.[10] Sev Necati started the social enterprise Women and Young People's Safety Solutions as a result of a deep concern for lack of safety considerations for the sector.[11]

In many instances, the pursuit of a socially directed mission shapes its core strategy and applied methodologies.[12] For instance, the National Foundation for Teaching Entrepreneurship (NFTE), in carrying out its mission, takes eight specific steps: (a) developing dynamic curricula, (b) training teachers and young professionals, (c) partnering with schools and communities, (d) building on volunteerism, (e) linking classroom experiences with the real world, (f) offering support service to program graduates, (g) providing research frameworks, and (h) expanding public awareness.[13]

The process of social entrepreneurship is different from traditional commercial enterprises because their primary objective is based on a social desire to "do good" rather than to exclusively seek profit.[14] There exists a deep desire for meaning and purpose. At the end of the day, a social enterprise is measured by the contributions it makes and the results that come about.[15]

Ultimately, an international social entrepreneur's ability to deliver social changes lies in possessed competencies, networks, and personal inclinations. For instance, in initiating the Drug-Free America campaign, Phillip Joanous, the chairman of advertising agency Dailey & Associates, tapped into his broad experience in media advertising to highlight the endemic issue of drug abuse in the country. After realizing that solving the drug problem in the country requires widespread social awareness and attitudinal changes, he sought the support of the American Association of Advertising Agencies. Through a joint effort with the agency, he launched an intense advertising campaign that heightened public awareness of the risks and consequences of drug abuse.[16]

An understanding of the issues and careful assessment of the value of a contribution is important. Joanous identified his mission after learning about the incidence of drug abuse in the country and its causes and implications. He knew the underlying environment and cared deeply about its potential consequences to society. He then proceeded to utilize his competencies, networks, time, and resources to initiate social change.

As the international social entrepreneur develops a vision and mission agenda, the ability to add value[17] and acquire resources[18] has to be considered. In general, entrepreneurs require appropriate information, specialized abilities, capital, and manpower resources to successfully initiate their ventures.[19] The selected mission has to attract capital. Securing finance is an obstacle for social enterprises, and the fear of not securing finance is a barrier to entry.[20] Sev Necati of the social enterprise Women and Young People's Safety Solutions alluded to the need for early access to funding and grant resources.[21]

Vision formation is critical because it becomes a framework for success and sets the stage for overcoming future problems [22] There needs to be clarity of purpose.[23]Authors Sandra Waddock and James Post highlight the fact that the formulated vision is essential for social entrepreneurs due to the complexity of circumstances, the saliency of the issues, and the strong support required from other participants as the venture is implemented.[24]

Along with vision development, the social issue has to be "framed" clearly in the minds of all "stakeholders"—organizational members, sponsors, partners, as well as the community. Author Archie Carroll describes "stakeholders" as "any individual or group who can affect or is affected by the actions, decisions, policies, practices or goals of the organization."[25] The targeted social issue must be considered important by all stakeholders, and the merits should be highlighted in order that action may be carried out.[26]

A well-developed and strategically positioned vision leads to wide support by stakeholders. Citizens within a society actually seek the sharing of a vision and value systems.[27] The support and participation of parties and active participants expedites action and allows the vision to grow and flourish. At times, followers and supporters of the vision develop levels of commitment and empowerment that parallel that of the original founder:[28] "The mission's core values is critical in uniting the team and moving everyone passionately toward the same goal."[29]

The conversion of vision into action, strategic utilization of resources, and the formation of a viable agenda[30] are critical for the success of social enterprises. In pursuing a mission of supporting high-impact entrepreneurs in emerging markets, social enterprise Endeavor strategically selected locations where it could make a significant impact. Then, the organization carefully planned implementation modes and leveraged available resources and networks to achieve its mission. This combined set of measures led to the attainment of an excellent social development platform.

An organization's vision and mission have to be maintained and kept consistent over time. There is a risk that the firm might steer away from its original mission:[31] "Mission creep is a key challenge for social enterprises."[32] Social enterprises have to stay true to what they stand for;[33] social entrepreneurs need to stay motivated: "Long term motivation is a major challenge for social enterprises . . . (social entrepreneurs) may start out on social enterprises and end up running charities—this is disheartening. Social problems don't go away, motivation can."[34] Studies suggest that social entrepreneurs can feel disillusioned over time, fear failure, and become frustrated in their chosen career.[35]

Due to evolving market conditions, the way a mission is carried out needs to be fine-tuned. It is important to consistently develop cost advantages, explore unmet needs and underserved sectors, provide emphasis on quality and service mix, and consider timing issues.[36] Modification of operational structure is necessary.[37] Heightened transparency and simplification of systems offer countless benefits.[38] Pricing adjustments need to be made. Strategically pricing in order to optimize returns positively impacts profitability.[39] Over time, social enterprises have to refine their portfolios to nurture products with financial, social, and strategic value and to eliminate those that have a low-mission fit and that are not sustainable.[40] Social enterprises should be focused on their missions and strategies, while adjusting to a changing environment.[41]

In carrying out their missions, social enterprises find foreign locations attractive. Many private corporations have been drawn to emerging international frontiers, and social enterprises are not an exception. This trend will likely continue in the future, as there is a need to shift social service paradigms from domestic to international. It is evident that globalization converges social issues. For instance, challenges relating to environmental degradation, AIDS, poverty, epidemics, drugs, human trafficking, crime, and corruption transcend borders. These issues are both local and global. They are a cause of concern for every single global citizen, and they require active participation on the part of international social entrepreneurs.

Engaged in a typical business enterprise, the international social entrepreneur's ability to spot the right opportunity is important. The suitable opportunity is a confluence of factors such as issue relevance; alignment with the set vision and mission; skills and competencies; and access to resources. The ability of an international social entrepreneur to select the optimal situation and make a judgment call is important.

International social entrepreneurs are self-motivated and are driven to change the world where they can: "Social entrepreneurs are driven . . . and socially motivated."[42] In selecting an appropriate vision and mission, international social entrepreneurs need to personally evaluate themselves as well as their organizational competencies. Consideration of past experiences, skills, and networks are relevant, as these would have an impact on the speed, breadth, and efficiency of business execution.

Conclusion

Finding a unique area where real value can be added is key. After all, social entrepreneurs are described as precursors of change through the creation of social value, innovation, and parsimonious adaptation.[43] They possess a strong desire to build social capital through concept enhancement, introduction of new methodologies, and management systems.[44] A keen awareness of one's purpose, competencies, and potential contribution to change sets the stage for the formation and pursuit of the international social entrepreneur's mission.

CHAPTER 5

Plan for Internationalization

People are always blaming their circumstances for what they are. I don't believe in circumstances. The people who get on in this world are the people who get up and look for the circumstances they want, and, if they can't find them, make them.

—George Bernard Shaw

Tommy Hutchinson has made a profound impact on social entrepreneurs worldwide. He started a company called i-genius, which is an online social network that connects members in over 90 countries. The website encourages partnerships and collaboration between social entrepreneurs, companies, media, government, and nongovernment organizations. It also hosts social entrepreneurship summits and events. Simple, practical, and yet profound, the company has made an impact on many lives.[1]

Whatever the line of business, profit or nonprofit, one of the most dynamic business events in recent years pertains to how enterprises internationalize. In fact, there has been a growing research interest in firm internationalization. In the case of social enterprises, venture internationalization has grown in popularity. Companies that internationalize can make widespread international impacts. For instance, in just a few years, i-genius has reached out to over 90 countries.

After a social enterprise identifies its mission, planning a mode of internationalization is a logical next step. Some social enterprises are driven to internationalize early, and even immediately, while others opt to take more time developing the domestic concern. Either option works, depending on what the enterprise goals are.

There are several internationalization opportunities. An International Franchise Association report indicated that about 400 firms franchise internationally yearly and are predominant in sectors such as service, training, education, health care, technology, food service, and retail.[2]

Anecdotal evidence points to the successful international expansion of social enterprises. As an example, the National Foundation for Teaching

Entrepreneurship, a social enterprise engaged in providing entrepreneurship training for low-income youth, successfully utilized licensing arrangements to expand into several international locations.[3]

International social entrepreneurs create innovative business models as they expand into foreign markets. For instance, David Green started the Aravind Eye Hospital in India to provide hundreds of affordable eye surgeries each year. Utilizing a business model that played on economies of scale and self-sustainability, he was able to provide most services for free or below cost. Through the model he created, he was able to generate extra revenue to sustain the business. His success allowed him to undertake expansion in several countries. He has since replicated the business model in different international locations, including Nepal, Malawi, Egypt, Guatemala, El Salvador, Tibet, Tanzania, and Kenya.[4]

Through the implementation of revolutionary approaches, international social entrepreneurs are redefining traditional practices and are transforming countries. A company called Advance Aid, founded by David Dickie and Simon Lucas, decided to focus on the social issue of slow international relief. During international disasters, lack of both logistics planning and preparation often delays the arrival of critical supplies. Advance Aid facilitates the prompt mobilization of relief resources by positioning stocks in warehouses in high-risk locations. As a result of their model, when disasters strike in needy nations, relief goods are ready for quick mobilization. Their international presence has helped create jobs, has attracted several corporate sponsors and supporters, and, more importantly, has improved delivery time of relief resources.[5]

International social enterprises tailor fit their international agenda to suit market requirements. YouthBuild is present in international locations such as South Africa, Mexico, Guatemala, El Salvador, Nicaragua, Honduras, Haiti, Jamaica, Canada, Serbia, Scotland, Israel, Bangladesh, Vietnam, India, Sri Lanka, Timor, China, Zambia, Indonesia, and West Bank-Gaza. The organization has a different emphasis in each of the locations they work in. For instance, in Zambia, they emphasized the creation of an employment fund; in Sri Lanka, livelihood in rural areas; and in Serbia, training initiatives for technology and conflict management.[6] While they follow a general mission and agenda for development, the company is prepared to make refinements to better respond to the needs of their target sector.

Since many social enterprises are internationalizing, there is value in revisiting international trade definitions, theories, concepts, and ideas to identify viable approaches. Internationalization is defined as a firm's external move toward foreign shores.[7] It refers to income generation or operational expansion outside of the company's domestic market.[8] Studies suggest that internationalization is driven by an individual[9] or by a major mover within the enterprise. Social enterprise internationalization therefore takes place as a result of the intent of the founder or a member of the management team.

A key consideration in the internationalization process is identifying what markets are suitable and the appropriate ways of entering those markets.[10]

In striving to understand the internationalization process, it is important to assess a firm's motivation. *Why should firms internationalize? What benefit would it offer the social enterprise or international social entrepreneur?* Research suggests that economics is a major rationalization due to efficient resource utilization,[11] transaction gains,[12] as well as financial efficiencies.[13] Many firms internationalize because of perceived gains. For social enterprises, the potential expansion of the double bottom line and the resulting social and profit impacts are motivators for internationalization.

Social enterprises internationalize in different ways. This is largely due to influences brought about by individual and organizational factors. Research studies suggest that a firm's behavior drives internationalization.[14] For instance, an individual's motivation,[15] strategic actions in dealing with changes,[16] responses to market factors,[17] and entrepreneurial disposition[18] shape the extent of firm internationalization.

In the course of internationalization, entrepreneurial behavior varies and also affects future courses of action. Author Svante Andersson alluded to three types of entrepreneurs in the context of internationalization: (a) technical—focused on product or service innovations or technologies; (b) structural—anchored in organizational forms and frameworks that reshape business dynamics; and (c) marketing oriented—those that implement marketing initiatives in new territories or geographical regions.[19] The type of entrepreneurial attitude possessed by the international social entrepreneur and the social enterprise management team shapes the path toward internationalization.

The speed of internationalization is influenced by possessed entrepreneurial attitudes. Authors Susan Freeman and Tamer Cavusgil identified four entrepreneurial attitude states conducive to accelerated internationalization (rated from low to high extent of adaptive behavior and personal interaction): (a) responder, (b) opportunist, (c) experimentalist, and (d) strategist.[20] In their view, the "strategist" tends to implement actions with a higher extent of adaptability and personal interaction. Internationalizing social enterprises that utilize this approach likely gain more traction in their internationalization efforts.

The composition of a management team has an impact on internationalization. Social enterprises need full team commitment to achieve their goals.[21] Factors such as managerial mind-sets[22] and team diversity[23] shape the breadth and scope of internationalization. A social enterprise with a team of executives with multicultural backgrounds would likely be more open to internationalization than one that is entirely monocultural.

When considering internationalization, business enterprises respond to external forces and change propagators.[24] Oftentimes, a strong impetus drives foreign investment.[25] For instance, in the home country, environmental shifts,[26] government policies,[27] industry conditions,[28] and institutional arrangements[29] motivate firms to explore opportunities overseas. In the host country, factors such as entry barriers,[30] cultural disparity,[31] government policies,[32] degree of market divergence from the home country,[33] and institutional frameworks[34] shape investment interests. As business organizations, social enterprises are exposed to the same factors.

Aside from external influences, the key to international expansion lies within the firm and the attributes it possesses. Based on gathered research, five key organizational attributes seal the fate of firm internationalization. These factors are *organization, technology and knowledge, organizational relationship, management execution*, and *strategic direction*. *Organization* attributes refer to characteristics that determine how a firm organizes itself in terms of structure and size. *Technology and knowledge* attributes refer to characteristics pertaining to the know-how of the firm and the tools they possess that allow business functions to be carried out. *Organizational relationship* attributes pertain to the networks and other firm associations the firm possesses as it carries out its business. *Management execution* attributes refer to how the firm implements its activities. *Strategic direction* attributes refer to the overall plan of action and strategy that the firm has put together in order to achieve its goals. Figure 5.1 illustrates the five organizational attributes in relation to the firm's internationalization.

Figure 5.1. Relationship between firm attributes and internationalization.

The following section describes each of the organizational attributes and their impact on internationalization.

Organization

The way a firm is organized, including its people and organizational architecture, provides a framework for behavior and action as the firm internationalizes.

Corporate history. Research suggests that a firm's past shapes its mindset and how it organizes itself. Organizational "imprinting" refers to a scenario where a firm's early experiences shape its future course.[35] For instance, a social enterprise that lost money in an emerging market expansion may be discouraged from expanding further. It may decide to stay focused on domestic markets for several years. In the same manner, environmental conditions and firm experiences lead firms to behave in certain ways. It has been observed that due to their exposure to unstable political environments, some multinational firms are more prepared to succeed in diverse business terrains.[36] The social enterprise Endeavor commenced operations in challenging emerging nations. This exposure has prepared them for success in similar markets.[37]

Firm predisposition. Partly due to team chemistry, employee backgrounds and mind-sets, and industry conditions, firms tend to be predisposed to behave in certain manners. Social enterprises that have recruited diverse employees would likely end up being more open-minded toward internationalization. Firms that internationalize early in their growth hold positive attitudes toward internationalization[38] and are more adaptable[39] than more traditional firms.

Organizational set-up. Due to the diversity of business forms and arrangements, social enterprises that internationalize utilize different organizational models. Social enterprises have to assess their organizational readiness.[40] Some enterprises have more resources in place to undertake international expansion. Social enterprises have to deal with organizational barriers and challenges, such as use of incentives, organizational culture, team factors, and recruitment policies.[41] In addition, bureaucracy needs to be minimized so the firm can be nimble and aggressively capture opportunities.[42] Innovative organizational forms are commonly used in the internationalization process.[43] In Ghana, Arizona State University initiated a social enterprise known as Global Resolve, creatively partnered with local schools, to improve water and energy conditions in the country.[44]

Size. Size disparities lead to diverse firm capabilities and organizational priorities. Larger firms have more manpower resources to pursue opportunities when compared to smaller or newer ones. Larger firms have a higher propensity for export.[45] Research shows, however, that size is not a deterrent to the pursuit of international trade initiatives.[46] Social enterprises optimize social networks by tapping into volunteers to further their agendas. For instance, the Kramden Institute has over 1,000 volunteers.

Management team composition. The extent of diversity in a management team has an impact on the firm's internationalization. Studies indicate that top-management diversity results in a heightened ability to internationalize.[47] It is important to cultivate human and relational capital[48] and to facilitate the exchange of viewpoints held by the management team to thoroughly assess potential internationalization.[49] Endeavor has been active in the practice of international social entrepreneurship. Endeavor's board is comprised of successful individuals from diverse backgrounds. The company's current chairman is Edgar Bronfman, Jr., CEO of the Warner Music Group. James Wolfensohn, the former president of the World Bank, is also a member of the board. The company has invited several venture capitalists, bankers, and industry leaders to join their team.

Organizational diversity. Aside from the diversity of employees and the management team, the extent to which a company has diversified its international presence has business implications. The quantification of how many locations a foreign business operation has is defined as its international diversity.[50] This diversity leads to several organizational merits such as the gaining of technological knowledge.[51] Partners in Health has benefited from technological and research gains in their multicountry operations.

Entrepreneurial disposition. Firms differ with regard to their entrepreneurial interests, inclinations, and capabilities. Research has demonstrated the impact of entrepreneurship on firm growth[52] and profitability.[53] Entrepreneurship plays a significant role in the internationalization process.[54] Social enterprises with highly entrepreneurial members would more likely internationalize than those lacking such members.

There are several factors that shape how a firm is organized. These factors can determine the social enterprise's international success. It is relevant for social enterprises to examine these organizational factors and to assess the firm's level of preparedness for internationalization. Understanding areas of strengths and weaknesses helps in the planning and execution of strategies.

Technology and Knowledge

The know-how and information possessed by a firm shapes its ability to survive and prosper in foreign locations. It also indicates what added values a firm can offer and leverage overseas.

Knowledge optimization and learning. Knowledge gained over time impacts internationalization[55] and factors into the processes[56] involved in achieving internationalization and certain modes of entry into foreign markets.[57] Firms learn in different ways, and their learning experiences vary.[58] For instance, previous learning gained from domestic markets,[59] network formation,[60] and internationalization[61] better prepares a firm for overseas expansion. International learning heightens firm performance[62] and enhances adaptability.[63] It is beneficial for internationalizing firms to cultivate global thinking in their organization,[64] to optimize knowledge in order to strengthen competitive edge,[65] and to collaborate with other entities[66] in order to strengthen their knowledge pool. Many social enterprises draw upon lessons learned in international markets to define future strategies.

Use of research and information. Internationalizing firms need to gather prompt and accurate information in order to make informed decisions: "Research is essential in the internationalization process."[67] Access to the right information helps determine which markets are ideal for market entry.[68] Research suggests that knowledge of markets is shaped by the social ties possessed by the firm.[69] Endeavor recruits top MBA students from leading U.S. schools to partner with their selected entrepreneurs in emerging markets.

Use of technology. Internationalizing firms should have the ability to use technology wisely. Kiva.org developed a website that is understandable across cultures. In the case of Internet firms, the web traffic they attract and the images they project have an impact on their internationalization efforts.[70] Adaptation and flexibility are always necessary. Many web-based firms have locally adapted websites.[71] Technology is a key part of internationalization, since it allows firms to highlight their strengths and competencies. In the same manner, as firms expand in foreign locations, they are also in a position to expand their technological knowledge[72] and to learn. Many social enterprises have taken what they have learned in emerging markets and applied them to other locations.

Technology clearly factors into the internationalization effort. Evaluation of a firm's technological readiness and factoring technology in the firm's strategic planning are relevant considerations.

Organizational Relationship

A firm's ability to use its networking skills and the types of relationships it builds affects its ability to internationalize.

Networking ability. Internationalizing firms are different in regard to their intent and ability to network. Research suggests that networks[73] and interorganizational linkages[74] tend to facilitate internationalization. Endeavor developed strong partnerships with academic institutions, media groups, and government entities in countries they operate in.

Firm relationships. Strategic use of a firm's social capital heightens a firm's competitive edge in the internationalization process.[75] There are merits in the integration of human and relational capital.[76] Factors such as connections,[77] relationships and networks,[78] and partnering activities[79] are documented as facilitating the internationalization process. A firm's relationship-building capabilities subsequently impact its business, since they play a hand in knowledge acquired,[80] international partner selection,[81] and prompt execution of strategy.[82] Common indicators of firm relationships are international collaborations[83] and strategic alliances.[84] Social enterprises have to collaborate with others, engage in partnerships, and interact with customers.[85] When expanding into South Africa, YouthBuild's relationships with various organizations were helpful. The company worked hand in hand with the Umsobomvu Youth Fund (UYF), the South Africa Department of Housing, Habitat for Humanity, the city of Johannesburg, the Institute for Education, and Training for Industry to launch the YouthBuild facility in Ivory Park. This facility subsequently provided countless youth with opportunities to build houses.

The manner in which firms build relationships also factors into internationalization success. Clearly, some firms are endowed with more talent and resources than others. Some firms need to emphasize organizational relationships in their line of business more than others. All firms, however, utilize relationships in one form or the other. In the case of international social enterprises, a clear understanding of how organizational relationships affect the planned agenda is important. Preparing and executing a detailed strategic plan on relationship development creates a distinct organizational advantage.

Management Execution

The way in which a management team executes its action agenda factors into its internationalization efforts.

Managing risk. Some firms are better than others in assessing and managing risks associated with overseas expansion. Some firms also take a more aggressive stance toward risk than others. There are companies that look at foreign expansion as a way of spreading their risk across locations.[86] Social enterprises may gain by diversifying revenue sources.[87] The real estate firm Enterprise Community Partners pursued the goal of developing houses for low-income communities.[88] Their approach may have been viewed as a high-risk pursuit by many; however, through sound management and strategic development, the enterprise mitigated risk, became highly profitable, and helped many people own homes.

Agility. Both the stage of international expansion and the speed of internationalization vary from firm to firm. Some firms internationalize early in their growth cycle.[89] These firms are said to be "born global," as they start to internationalize in 2 to 6 years after formation.[90] In their internationalization, these firms select foreign locations with close "psychic distance" and do not significantly differ from their home-country markets.[91] In the case of U.S.-based social enterprise Girls on the Run, their first international location was Canada.[92] The location was geographically close, culturally similar, and potentially more manageable in the company's viewpoint.

Communication ability. The ability to communicate is an important attribute for internationalizing firms. Information flows impact the "psychic distance" from market to firm and from firm to market.[93] A firm's ability to translate clear and efficient messages across several stakeholders presents added advantages. In Endeavor's operations in emerging markets, they make a point of working closely with media such as radio, television, newspapers, and magazines to highlight the success stories of entrepreneurs they have supported.

Financial competitiveness and preparedness. Internationalizing firms need to manage financial resources, as there are set-up costs, monitoring, and product modifications associated with overseas market entry.[94] Multinational corporations use an acquisition strategy to gain competitive strength.[95] Research studies point to the financial merits of firm internationalization, including heightened chances of survival,[96] income stability,[97] and increase in profitability.[98] Firm profitability in a new environment is shaped by factors such as rivalry, potential of entrants, possibility of product substitution, ability of suppliers to bargain, and ability of buyers to bargain.[99] Social enterprises need to pay attention to cash flow and to carefully consider how customer needs are met.[100] It is sensible to look at all cost angles and to understand the break-even point, product value and its impact on pricing, and the impact of price on firm profitability.[101] In its African operations, KickStart selects products and approaches that provide the optimum financial return for the amount of time and labor invested.

Flexibility. The ability to respond to foreign market conditions is important for internationalizing firms. Internationalizing firms should learn to deal with uncertainty[102] and to be flexible.[103] Research has shown that in the process of internationalization, smaller firms are more flexible than larger ones.[104] Social enterprises gain through innovation and experimentation.[105] World of Good implemented a diversity of projects in several locations across Africa. In South Africa, they built a computer laboratory; in Swaziland, they emphasized literacy; and in Tanzania, they worked on sanitation.

Control. Despite numerous complexities associated with the internationalization process, firms need to stay in control:[106] "Controlled and managed growth is a key challenge for social enterprises."[107] In the case of Ten Thousand Villages, even with operations in 38 countries, they make an effort to support and collaborate with their artisans to solve problems and to enhance design and product quality.

In the course of internationalization, the way management executes their tasks evidently varies. There are tasks that the organization executes more efficiently than others. It is important for social enterprises to identify which tasks are critical to their internationalization success and to consider these in the planning efforts. For instance, if managing risk is a primary consideration and the management team lacks the competency for its execution, it would make sense to take specific actions such as hiring an additional manager specialized in risk management, providing risk management training, hiring a risk consultant, or utilizing a risk assessment tool. Planning ahead and prioritizing the agenda heightens the chances for success.

Strategic Direction

The strategic approaches and direction implemented by an internationalizing firm sets the path toward success or failure.

Leveraging and gaining competitive edge. The ways in which firms leverage their resources is critical in the internationalization process. Aside from their product offerings, firms possess nontangible assets such as know-how, proprietary information and materials, and corporate image.[108] Organizational skills and experiences are important assets.[109] Organizational resources, along with the product lines, have to be unique in order to be leveraged in a successful way internationally.[110] An excellent product or service helps overcome the challenges of foreignness.[111] In Paraguay, local consumer lenders responded aggressively to new social enterprise entrants by implementing unorthodox marketing strategies.[112] Quality products that are differentiated from other competitors helps build a competitive advantage, and such products are critical in foreign markets.[113] When developing strategy, leveraging should be considered alongside product and business lines[114] and across a diversity of stakeholders.[115] Leveraging is best pursued across several locations[116] and in a sustainable fashion. Authors Gary Hamel and C. K. Prahalad recommend that when seeking a competitive edge, firms need to (a) tap into niches in foreign markets, (b) leverage resources to take advantage of scope and scale, and (c) frame their products on a global scale.[117] KickStart has emphasized the importance of quality and brand for the internationalizing social enterprise.[118]

Corporate posturing. The ways that firms position themselves in international markets is an important consideration. Some firms need to internationalize to build their image and credibility.[119] Social enterprises should have transparent systems and should build trust through formal and informal mechanisms.[120] Both Ten Thousand Villages and KickStart attest to the importance of properly framing an organization's corporate position in the mind-sets of consumers.

Strategic growth and expansion. In an effort to grow and expand, firms implement a diversity of strategies. Social enterprises benefit by creating teams that focus on strategic planning.[121] Many business decisions are based on organizational inclinations and priorities. Firms expand overseas to access new markets and to retain market shares,[122] to acquire new entities,[123] and to respond to industry, competitive, and institutional factors.[124] A firm's combined organizational approach that allow it to deal with issues such as acquisitions, divestitures, alliances, and resource utilization is referred to as its dynamic capability.[125] Architectural capability refers to combined action and resource utilization employed by a firm that allows it to grow and to be productive.[126] When internationalizing, companies take on organizational transformations, such as the revamping of their accounting and human resource functions, to respond to opportunities and challenges.[127] Social enterprises need to reevaluate plans and strategies:[128] "Many social enterprises need to develop a well detailed strategic plan."[129]

The overall strategic direction of a firm determines its internationalization success. Understanding its strengths and weaknesses and taking appropriate action are important considerations. In identifying viable strategies, social enterprises have to be prepared to look at the big picture and to assess how the organization fits in the broader operational environment.

Conclusion

It is evident that there are several factors that shape international entry. Social enterprises and international social entrepreneurs need to carefully think about and plan for internationalization. Some social enterprises end up failing in a certain geographic location or related business segment. Other social enterprises use income generated from a specific segment or market to subsidize a poorer performing one.[130]

A well-balanced internationalization that meets a firm's desired double bottom line is essential. Social enterprises have to assess external and internal influences and gauge the impact that these influences have in the internationalization process. They should look closely at their existing organization in order to understand its capabilities, its competencies, and potential challenges to its internationalization.

Many social enterprises have succeeded internationally and were rewarded by gaining high profitability and making a meaningful social impact.

There are several lessons to be learned from successful social enterprises. For instance, Endeavor enters emerging nations that are poised toward growth. They select local partners to develop country boards and affiliates and to ensure early commitment of partners. They also conduct research and thorough assessment of target markets.

Furthermore, in selecting international locations for expansion, Endeavor utilizes a five-point criteria: (a) location has enabling framework in the form of strong macroeconomic conditions; (b) location has scalability (i.e., a large number of target markets); (c) location has pull in the form of a high level of interest from local affiliates; (d) management feasibility—due consideration is given to the existing organizational structure and mode of implementation, including issues such as language, flights, and time zones; and (e) mission congruence—preference is placed on locations where a significant impact may be made.[131]

A well-conceived international plan that is true to a social enterprise's mission, goals, and capabilities provides a framework for successful internationalization.

CHAPTER 6

Pursue Strategic Action

We are blind until we see
That in the human plan
Nothing is worth the making
If it does not make the man
Why build these cities,
If man unbuilded goes?
In vain we build the world
Unless the builder also grows.

—Edwin Markham

Despite being born in an isolated territory in Argentina, Wenceslao Casares did not allow geography to limit his dreams and actions. Casares capitalized on the Internet as a medium through which to reach out to thousands of people. He established a personal finance site called Patagon.com and pioneered online trading in Argentina. Patagon became a leading financial services site in Latin America. Eventually, Casares sold 75% of the business to Banco Santander for $529 million. He stayed on as chief executive of the company and further expanded the venture into Portugal, Spain, and the United States. He has carried out an active role in a company called Endeavor, which nurtures young entrepreneurs in emerging markets. Seeing the need to further financial know-how in Latin America, he has pursued education initiatives geared toward training students in basic financial and investment concepts.[1] In the case of Wenceslao Casares, then, the insights gained and methodologies learned in a previous venture were integrated into the core strategy of a new socially directed pursuit.

In today's global society, there are numerous opportunities to integrate new technologies and concepts in viable social enterprises. A social entrepreneur's ability to crystallize ideas and concepts and to tie them together to plan and implement strategic action are key considerations in the development of social enterprises: "Strategic thinking is an important attribute for social entrepreneurs."[2]

Since there is a constant need to manage the complex interplay of forces that affect socially inspired actions and behaviors in the market, a well-orchestrated strategy is relevant.[3] International social enterprises should consider site, process, and human investments.[4] International social entrepreneurs have to balance diverse factors that affect the business and engage in careful planning and thinking. It takes strategic thinking for a company like Aurolab, a manufacturer of intraocular lenses that sell for over \$150 in industrialized nations, to sell similar units for \$4 in developing nations.[5]

The international social entrepreneur's chosen set of actions impacts businesses and economies. Studies suggest that decentralized actors play a critical role in a state's economic development.[6] Philanthropically oriented private enterprises have a role in a society's democratic health.[7] The goal of social enterprise Mercy Corps to support microfinance firms in emerging markets has the potential to impact the lives of millions.

In considering strategies for international social entrepreneurs, operational models need to be assessed. Author Alan Fowler identified two models in the practice of social entrepreneurship: (a) integration— through the intersection of profit generating activities and social causes, and (b) reinterpretation—through creative expansion by lowering costs and spreading outcomes.[8] In the integrated approach, the social enterprise strategically weaves social and business systems to optimize profit gains. The reinterpretation approach builds on economies of scale and scope to optimize business output. In their quest for business development, many social enterprises have been innovative. Nonprofit and for-profit organizational hybrids exist.[9] For instance, nonprofit organizations have engaged in social franchises or the franchising of socially directed ventures. According to Billy Shore, chairman of Community Wealth Ventures, "Social franchises offer yet another option for nonprofits willing to leverage assets in the interest of the revenue generation needed to expand their mission."[10] A diversity of other organizational models is utilized in international social entrepreneurship expansions.

Aside from having to use the most suitable organizational structure, international social entrepreneurs should have an ability to identify challenges ahead of time. In the case of nongovernmental development organizations, countless challenges exist as concept development and expansions are carried out.[11] Anticipating and planning through challenges is essential.

International social entrepreneurs have to deal with a "multiplexity" of challenges.[12] In the course of internationalization, social enterprises should work and collaborate with several individuals and entities. For instance, starting a social enterprise in an emerging nation means extensive discussions and joint planning with constituents, partners, local managers, customers, sponsors, government officials, media, and nongovernment organizations, among others. With several interorganizational interfaces, the potential for friction and problems escalates. Social enterprises, therefore, have to be prepared to address issues affecting the needs of multiple stakeholders.

When faced with complex issues and potential challenges, careful planning and the proper execution of strategic action are essential. An example of a small organization that pursued strategic action is one owned by Martin Morales in Mexico. In this country, exotic birds are often caught in the wild and illegally exported to other countries. As more individuals participated in the trade, some of the rare bird species experienced a sharp drop in population. In Mexico, however, it is legal to export exotic birds as long as they are bred in captivity.[13] Seeing this is an opportunity to converge revenue generation and social responsibility, Morales formed an organization for bird farmers that addressed five social issues: (a) income for himself and the community, (b) prevention of illegal activity, (c) better care for the environment, (d) expansion of bird management skills across the country, and (e) response to an international market demand for exotic pets.

When international social entrepreneurs execute their strategies correctly, they are in the position to become catalysts for change.[14] Victoria Hale, chairman and founder of One World Health, aimed to create the first nonprofit pharmaceutical company in the United States. By utilizing innovative research methodologies, and by specializing in niche segments that allow for significant impacts, her company is on its way to successfully combating major ailments around the world. Many social enterprises have the potential to redefine the economic, business, and social dimensions of a society.

International social entrepreneurs benefit from leveraging unique competencies and targeting specific markets. Small firms can compete with large organizations and overcome deficiencies in resources when niche markets are pursued and key competencies are capitalized on.[15] For instance, child and family wellness (CFW) shops that quickly expanded across Kenya distributed quality health products and services to remote locations that needed them.[16]

International social entrepreneurs have to be experts in collaborating and rallying for support. Social enterprises need to build on the understanding and support of the local citizenry.[17] Strategic selection of the appropriate cooperating networks and support groups is important. Many social enterprises succeeded internationally as a result of the proper selection of partners. In foreign countries, clusters within communities exist.[18] A cluster with stronger and tighter networks has the potential to carry out a mission more effectively than another. There is a potential for social enterprises to effectively build on these clusters to expand their business. Similarly, contacts are critical to this process,[19] and the ability to rally support and build from organizational clusters offers a gateway to success.[20] When social enterprises band together, synergies are built and the potential for success increases. For instance, the social enterprise Strategic Employment Solutions was created as a partnership between six nonprofit groups that intended to provide employment for the disabled.[21]As they joined forces and brought together diverse skills and abilities, a stronger and more effective organization was formed.

International social entrepreneurs have to be prepared to work with a diversity of mind-sets and attitudes. Across cultures there are variations in attitudes placed on trust[22] and relationships.[23] In some societies, females are constrained in their effort to build networks across male-dominated groups.[24] Differences in ways of thinking and doing business pose additional hurdles for internationalizing social enterprises. The ability to embrace diversity and work through its challenges is essential.

International social entrepreneurs have to be nimble and ready to adjust to unexpected changes. For instance, government funds may be cut, competition may intensify, and previously accessible grants may be reduced or eliminated.[25] Many social entrepreneurs, however, are equipped to respond to such challenges. They are, after all, characterized by their ability to plan for, and exercise, sound judgments.[26] However, they still need to be prepared to reevaluate plans and continually refine their strategies.[27]

International social entrepreneurs have to develop a strategic set of plans that are anchored in value creation. Author Alan Fowler emphasizes the need for social entrepreneurs to incorporate value-added components in their endeavors.[28] In creating a socially directed business plan, students at the University of Arizona developed one geared toward helping the elderly avoid financial scams and challenges.[29] Their concept certainly provided very high value to the target market they intended to serve.

International social entrepreneurs should frame their strategies in the context of entrepreneurship and sound business judgment. Research has pointed to the centrality of entrepreneurship in the strategic actions of social entrepreneurs. Some studies cite the use of a business-centered approach and the strategic utilization of alliances and partnerships,[30] while other studies stress propensities to use skills such as efficient resource mobilization, orientation toward results, operational efficiencies, and the use of effective managerial approaches.[31] Many social enterprises have been a success largely due to sound management approaches. In social enterprises, management skills drive business success.[32]

International social entrepreneurs have to refine their strategic agendas to respond to changing market conditions. Market characteristics, stakeholder mind-sets, and business modalities evolve and therefore require organizational adjustments. For instance, studies point to a shift in thinking in venture philanthropy endeavors and how organizations desire to pursue social change.[33] In the same manner, many social enterprises have been observed to engage in the experimentation of new systems,[34] processes, structures, and organizational alignments. For instance, cognizant of the popularity of video games, Pam Omidyar started Hopelab, a nonprofit organization that uses video games to address health challenges. One of their products is a game called Re-Mission. In the game, the player shoots and destroys cancer cells. Their system is said to have inspired patients to stick with their medication regimen. Noting the success, the company is exploring similar video-game therapies for other diseases.[35]

Practiced innovation in social entrepreneurship has transformed the business landscape. Changes that are taking place have led to new thinking in the private and public sectors. For instance, due to the pressure to enhance service deliveries, executives in the public sector are forced to undertake strategic measures that are in step with the new demands of society.[36] Several government organizations supported the Advance Aid enterprise that expedited the delivery of relief goods.

As social entrepreneurship has expanded internationally, a diversity of strategic measures have been implemented. The reality is that a good number of executed international strategies defy rationality.[37] Many companies select their markets in a nonsystematized manner.[38] Nevertheless, it is apparent that a company's internationalization efforts are integral to its overall strategy.[39]

There is value in understanding how companies implement their international strategies and determine which approaches would likely be viable. Gathered research in international strategy points to two overarching themes that characterize how companies implement their international strategies. One approach is *inner directed*, where efforts are aimed internally and toward the organization. This includes approaches such as how the firm organizes itself and manages the enterprise. The other approach is *outer directed*, where efforts are directed toward a broader external environment. This strategy includes measures taken to deal with the opportunities and challenges in a foreign location, such as competitive approaches, entry mode, and alliance formations, among others.

Inner Directed

Inner-directed strategies are actions implemented by a company internally in the course of internationalization. For internationalizing social enterprises, this refers to strategic actions directed at its own organization as it copes in a foreign country.

Control. A firm's ability to institute control measures is critical in the internationalization process.[40] Many firms heighten their business control[41] and set up monitoring systems[42] to thrive and succeed in foreign markets. Controlled and managed growth is essential to the social enterprise.[43]

Resource utilization. Firms need to carefully assess how they use their resources as they internationalize. A competitive edge may be gained by the creative use of resources in strategy formation.[44] DataDyne uses computer technology to enhance data collection in emerging markets. Their developed software and systems allow public health workers to efficiently process information and do away with laborious paper surveys. In rolling out their product internationally, the company received the support of international organizations such as the World Health Organization, the UN Foundation, and Vodafone Foundation.[45] Working with experienced and field-tested international groups allowed the company to devote their resources to their own competencies and thereby optimize productivity.

Financial planning. Organizations have to think through how they use their financial resources. Effective cost management can provide an added advantage.[46] For social enterprises, cash flow,[47] income generation,[48] and profit maximization[49] are key considerations. Finding finances can be a challenge for social enterprises. Sev Necati of Women and Young People's Safety Solutions points out that social enterprises typically require access to funding and grant resources.[50]

Organizational arrangement and enhancement. Many firms utilize innovative forms in the course of internationalization.[51] Research suggests that organizational measures such as team diversity,[52] training in global thinking,[53] and diversity in subsidiary operations[54] can aid in internationalization success. It is important, however, to consider team capacity and competencies as an international agenda is developed.[55] Pepin, Tanqueda, Baker and Associates, a consulting firm specialized in the nonprofit sector, indicated that socially directed enterprises need to work on organizational barriers and challenges in order to succeed.[56]

Profitability. Firms take on proactive measures to stay profitable in the course of internationalization. The pursuit of entrepreneurial gain is a key motivator.[57] After all, internationalization stabilizes a firm's earnings[58] and leads to an improved chance of business survival [59] Sheetal Mehta of the social enterprise Shivia points out that the company's vision has to be pursued in the context of profitability.[60]

Sustainability mind-set. In developing their internationalization strategy, firms also need to consider long-term business implications. "Social enterprises need to plan for strategic sustainability."[61] For instance, actions pertaining to sustainability of their capabilities,[62] and long-term commitment toward shaping consumer mind-sets and growing the industry, are important.[63]

Outer Directed

Outer-directed strategies refer to a firm's courses of action that respond to the external environment in which it operates. For internationalizing social enterprises, this refers to strategic actions directed outside the organization as it copes with a foreign country. Gathered research suggests a tendency toward two types of actions: *proactive*—actions geared toward an anticipation of a potential outcome; and *reactive*—actions taken as a response to prevailing market conditions.

Proactive Strategies

Several internationalizing firms take proactive action in dealing with the various forces in overseas locations. This is evident among social enterprises as well.

Niche tapping. Firms seeking to sell into foreign markets need to know the niche they are looking to tap into. A competitive edge is gained when a niche market is successfully tapped.[64] Some companies take on several niches within a market by diversifying their product offering.[65] World of Good aims to improve the lives of poverty-stricken girls and women worldwide. As the cause is fairly broad, they have decided to pursue a mission that emphasizes wage disparities. Although they had already defined their service product, they further refined their product by segmenting it to meet the needs of their target market. Subsequently, they developed fair-wage guides, living-wage projects, labor links, and even microgrants to better reach out to their specific target sectors in the international markets.[66]

Leveraging. Firms need to build on a unique advantage in order to leverage successfully in an international market.[67] Leveraging comes in the form of an excellent product or service offering,[68] or in the strategic use of resources to take advantage of scope and scale.[69] There are advantages to be gained when corporate strengths are leveraged into a foreign location[70] or across several countries.[71] KickStart leverages the products and technologies they developed to aid in the enhancement of agriculture in Africa. The company differentiated themselves by thinking beyond just a quality product. The company taps into other competencies it possesses in building economies of scale, distribution, and supply-chain management to make a significant impact in the region.[72]

Product positioning. It is critical for firms to be able to correctly frame their product image to their target consumers and across a global scale.[73] The product or service offering may require modification to suit new markets: "Research is important in internationalizing social enterprises . . . in the case of Girls on the Run, what key components of the curriculum apply and do not apply in other nations need to be assessed."[74]

Growth and development. Many firms choose internationalization as a pathway to growth[75] and to increase market strength.[76] In their effort to expand overseas, firms take on a vertical-expansion approach, describing a downstream relationship with the overseas location. A backward vertical approach describes a situation where the firm mobilizes assets to foreign shores to secure raw materials or inputs, while a forward vertical approach is where a firm mobilizes resources to distribute or sell products or services.[77] A firm's level of commitment to internationalization varies. In some cases, a horizontal approach is more suitable, and expansion takes place when a firm sets up a factory or facility in an overseas market to sell products at the same time as maintaining manufacturing facilities in the home country.[78] The pace of internationalization also varies. Some firms internationalize a step at a time,[79] while others develop aggressively and skip through the typical developmental stages.[80] A well-known internationalization model known, the Uppsala Model, named after its developers who were professors at the University of Uppsala in Sweden, recommends that international expansion be gradual and anchored on the firm's market commitment and knowledge.[81] Professor Freek Vermeulen of the London Business School suggests that successful international expansion should have four steps: (a) expand where the company can optimize known knowledge, (b) transfer competitive advantage strategically whether through greenfield investment or acquisition, (c) prepare to customize approaches to suit markets, and (d) assimilate quickly, then move to other opportunities.[82] For social enterprises, the consulting firm Pepin, Tranqueda, Baker and Associates suggests that close attention be placed on how customer needs are met.[83] In the case of KickStart, they aim to balance quality, cultural suitability, and sustainability as they expand product lines.[84]

Mode of entry. Mode of entry is an important strategic decision for multinational corporations.[85] A well-planned market entry leads to more favorable consequences.[86] Common entry modes include exporting, turnkey projects, licensing, franchising, joint ventures, and wholly owned subsidiaries. Wholly owned subsidiaries typically come in the form of greenfield investment, when a company builds a new one from scratch, or acquisition, when a company acquires another. Multinational corporations prefer acquisitions to greenfield investments.[87] Acquisitions speed up the internationalization process,[88] and many companies use this approach to gain competitive strength.[89] Criteria for acquisition targets typically include size, organizational culture compatibility, and proximity, among others.[90] Other firms participate in creative international alliances to become more competitive and enter new markets more quickly.[91] Multinational corporations tend to prefer global alliances.[92] Interest in firm internationalization has led to a proliferation of theories. The theory of eclectic paradigm indicates that specific advantages accrued to a firm encourage internationalization as other markets appear more attractive in a business development perspective.[93] The product life cycle theory points out that firms export abroad, set up production facilities overseas and then export back to the country where the product was originally made.[94] Professor Michael Porter of the Harvard Business School postulated that firm internationalization should be considered alongside four key factors in a country, namely, factor conditions (i.e., infrastructure, skills, capital); demand (i.e., market size); related and supporting industries; and organization, strategy, structure, and competition.[95] These theories form a strong foundation for a firm's mode-of-entry decision. Ultimately, the decision a firm takes on how to enter the market will shape its future course.[96] Social enterprises have several business models to choose from as they internationalize. Licensing and franchising are increasingly common expansion modes.[97] Billy Shore, chairman of the consulting firm Community Wealth Ventures, pointed out that "social franchising is a vital new funding stream for non-profits."[98] The National Foundation for Teaching Entrepreneurship has successfully utilized the licensing model for both domestic and international expansions.[99]

Timing of entry. When a firm enters a market, it is essential to respond to social, economic, and technological changes.[100] Some firms internationalize early to capture overseas opportunities[101] and gain exposure in foreign markets.[102] In some cases, it is a way to survive.[103] Firms that are referred to as being born global internationalize within 2 to 6 years of business formation.[104] There are several advantages and disadvantages associated with both early and late market entry. It is imperative for a firm to complete a careful assessment of what needs to be achieved along the lines of its set mission and goals. In the case of Husk Power Systems, a prompt decision to make an entry into the India market was appropriate. The company developed the technology to convert rice husks to biogas, which fuels small power plants. As electricity is a major problem in India, and the rice husk is in abundant supply, the company decided to make an immediate market entry.[105]

Creative alliances. The types of alliances that a firm enters into in the internationalization process factors into its future success. Research suggests that alliances increase the level of firm internationalization[106] and enhance resource mobilization and speed of action.[107] In the case of new firms, the right alliance paves the way for successful market entry, technology access, and enhancement of image.[108] Social enterprises benefit by forming alliances and partnerships.[109] The social enterprise Global Resolve partnered with schools, civic organizations, and foundations as they implemented their international projects.

Use of knowledge. The way a firm utilizes knowledge positively impacts its course of internationalization.[110] Some firms demonstrate an absorptive capacity, where they gain knowledge from overseas endeavors and use this knowledge to enhance corporate business endeavors.[111] Research suggests that knowledge gained by firms shapes the selected entry mode,[112] helps to determine which markets to expand in,[113] facilitates the adaptation to host-country conditions,[114] and enhances a firm's performance.[115] Firms can capitalize on knowledge by strengthening information-collection efficiencies[116] and by optimizing the use of knowledge to gain a competitive edge.[117] Partners in Health shares knowledge they have gained in several emerging market operations to combat international health challenges.

Local resource utilization. Modalities in which a firm utilizes local resources is a key consideration. For instance, firms can learn from the capabilities and expertise of firms situated within the new market.[118] Ten Thousand Villages works with artisans in 38 countries. The company closely collaborates and supports the artisans. Products that are jointly created by the firm and the artisans utilizing local resources are leveraged and successfully marketed worldwide.

It is evident that in the course of international expansion, firms need to be proactive. The extent to which a firm is proactive determines its success. There are several factors to consider in gauging a firms proactive ability. It is important to examine the firm's attributes and assess them alongside the operating environment. Firms have to determine strengths and weaknesses and identify attributes demanded in the operating environment. A specific plan to build on specific strengths and address key weaknesses is essential.

The outlined set of proactive strategic actions offers firms the opportunity to further their business agendas. However, other courses of action pertaining to the external environment require a reactive nature.

Reactive Strategies

Reactive strategies refer to courses of action that firms take in response to existing external market conditions.

Navigating external influences. An internationalizing firm has to take action to respond to industry, institutional, and organizational factors in overseas locations.[119] At times, these decisions are driven by psychic distance, the extent to which a target country is different from the home country in terms of culture, politics, education, and related factors.[120] The social enterprise Endeavor lobbied with local politicians, sought enhancement in banking systems, and even facilitated the creation of new organizations as they pursued their mission of promoting entrepreneurship in emerging markets.[121]

Product customization. Market conditions in overseas markets are different from the home country—as a result, products have to be modified:[122] "Social enterprises need to be cognizant of different regulations and legislation governing charities, not for profits and for profits with social objectives."[123]

Planning through the performance cycle. Firm internationalization tends to wax and wane over time. Firm and market conditions are among the several influencers that contribute to the changes. Firms have to strategize through these fluctuating performance cycles and identify an optimal internationalization threshold.[124] For example, a firm's existing managerial pool may allow the efficient management of ten subsidiaries in ten countries, but adding one or two more may lead to efficiency declines, causing the overall performance of the firm to suffer. Girls on the Run opted to keep their focus on domestic markets and neighboring Canada until they are fully satisfied with their domestic operational systems.[125]

Adaptation. Firms have to take on adaptation measures when internationalizing. For instance, Internet companies tend to have locally adapted websites to reach out to local audiences.[126] Firm flexibility is critical in the internationalization process.[127] Smaller firms exhibit more flexibility than larger ones.[128] Yet, whether big or small, firms need to be cognizant of the market environment and make suitable adaptations to evolving market conditions.[129] Endeavor had to adapt and innovate in several international locations in order to succeed in their mission.[130]

Risk management. Internationalizing firms have to take measures to manage risk. There are numerous issues dealing with uncertainty in overseas markets.[131] Some firms have established overseas presence to spread risks.[132] Social enterprises such as Vision Support Trading utilize formal business planning to manage risk. Limiting capital exposure by engaging in licensing and franchising, instead of setting up wholly owned subsidiaries, may help mitigate risk.[133]

Human resources optimization. Due to different market conditions overseas, human resource structure and operations need to be altered and adjusted. For instance, when developing outsourcing operations overseas, hiring additional personnel to deal with differences in time zones and language challenges may be essential. Furthermore, providing specialized training for outsourcing partners is important for maintaining certain standards. Social entrepreneurs tend to see the high relevance of human resource management in their operations. Social entrepreneurs Robert McEwan and Molly Barker stressed the relevance of people in personal correspondences with the author: "Social entrepreneurs need to have the ability to get along well with others, as well as to forgive others, because sooner or later everyone will trip and fall and everyone deserves a helping hand."[134] "How we treat one another, and the systems we create toward that end, is critical in uniting the team and moving passionately toward the set goals."[135] Whatever the course of action in human resources management, careful planning is necessary to ensure seamless collaboration with partners in overseas locations. When done right, a firm's social capital can provide a unique competitive advantage.[136]

Integrated approach. Integration of strategy is important for internationalizing firms. Research suggests that human and relational capital have to be well integrated in order to achieve optimal performance.[137] In measuring organizational success, an optimal combination of underlying factors should be considered and weighed.[138] This allows organizational planners to see the big picture and see how parts connect. When a firm internationalizes, its ability to engage in global strategic coordination is essential to its success.[139] Therefore, there is value in training executives in the essence of globalization and the global strategic thinking that goes with it.[140] In carrying out its international expansion, Endeavor developed clear and cohesive guidelines that considered enabling frameworks, scalability, pull forces, managerial feasibility, and mission congruence.[141] In attempting to put together the big picture, and to understand how interconnections take place, a more coherent plan is developed.

It is clear that the outlined reactive strategies are helpful approaches in the course of internationalization. There are benefits to be gained when a firm carefully assesses which attributes that they possess will allow them to best execute these strategies. In areas where essential attributes are missing, an improvement or development plan has to be executed. When the right mix of organizational attributes is present for a firm to execute its strategy, the likelihood for successful implementation is heightened.

Conclusion

With a broad range of factors affecting international business decisions, international social entrepreneurs need to invest time and effort in strategic planning. An examination of inner- and outer-directed factors deserve consideration. A clear and well-defined set of actions that fits an organization's mission should be pursued.

Despite having to deal with several challenges and obstacles, international social entrepreneurs should stay focused on their goals and develop the best strategies possible to achieve their missions. In international locations, there are vast opportunities in which to contribute to changes and social betterment. In the words of author Jan Pronk, "We have to make the world a home for everyone."[142]

International social entrepreneurs are in a position to transform the international community by implementing strategic actions that combine elements of value creation, entrepreneurship and innovation, adaptation, and social contribution.

CHAPTER 7

Adjustment and Reinvention

The greatest discovery of my generation is that man can alter his life simply by altering his attitude of mind.

—James Truslow Adams

In the case of William Browder, turning wrongs into rights might be an overly simplistic motto for him, but this is exactly what he claims to do in life. A BA in economics from the University of Chicago and an MBA from Stanford Business School set a solid framework for his career in finance. The typical roller-coaster ride in international finance led Browder to lose 90% of the value of his company, Hermitage Fund, at the height of the ruble crisis in Russia. However, he never gave up on the country of his grandmother's birth. He decided to live in Russia and initiate a crusade to identify the challenges relating to corporate governance in the country. Browder exposes corporate problems to the public, and then identifies solutions to nurse these companies back to health.[1]

William Browder has turned what many may view as a personal disaster into an opportunity. While pursuing this opportunity, he reinvented himself and endeavored to make a difference on foreign shores.

This case highlights the need for international social entrepreneurs to adjust and reinvent in order to succeed in a global world. Domestic and international social enterprises are reinventing their organizations and refining their operational methodologies. In some cases, creative thinking leads to positive results. For instance, the Fair Oaks Community Center in California offered office spaces, tax breaks, and government incentives in order to host more than 30 nonprofit ventures. The nonprofit ventures, in turn, dealt with diverse community issues and helped address countless social needs.[2]

Traditional firms and socially oriented ventures are actively seeking international opportunities in new ways.[3] Research suggests that many high technology companies are "born global," since they have been able to expand globally in a short period of time.[4] The corporate world has seen a shift in the level of market interest, from the traditional 5% richest market segment to a broader group consisting of the poorest 40% primarily situated in emerging nations.[5]

Many organizations are starting to realize that domestic success of developed concepts, products, and services can be successfully replicated in other parts of the world. Notable examples of successful international concept expansions of socially directed initiatives include Grameen Bank by Muhammad Yunus and the Ashoka organization by Bill Drayton. Grameen Bank started by providing microcredit to the poorest sectors of society in Bangladesh, and the concept was successfully replicated in several other countries.[6] The Ashoka organization provides support to social entrepreneurs in 48 countries and is making an impact on many communities.[7]

The pursuit of an international social entrepreneurship is a path filled with challenges. There are many instances of failure. For instance, a study pointed out that socially directed projects by development agencies originating in Europe have a sustainability rate of only about 15%.[8] As they develop their social enterprises, international social entrepreneurs need to weave through these difficulties and to adjust and reinvent. Research studies suggest that social enterprises face obstacles in several areas. These challenges include the factors described in the following paragraphs.

Poor private-sector participation. In some locations, the private sector may not be supportive and can derail set goals and development agendas. Poor participation by the private sector in diverse community issues can limit community well-being and growth:[9] "Social enterprises need to get others to buy-in."[10]

Financial challenges. Even in the early stages of development, social entrepreneurs are faced with financial pressures from financiers and sponsors:[11] "Dealing with money and access to finance is a key challenge."[12] Those who fund social enterprises tend to provide only a small percentage of needed capital.[13] Resource access through traditional channels is sometimes difficult to acquire.[14] Social enterprise ventures, especially nonprofit organizations, need external grants and funding sources to operate.[15] Oftentimes, financial pressures are brought about by conflicting forces relating to the organization's real mission and the financial requirements necessary to attain set goals.[16] Conflicting enterprise goals will impact how the venture will manage itself during testing times.[17] It is not easy for social enterprises to continually stay profitable.[18] For instance, due to a lackluster business performance, a social enterprise in the United Kingdom called Aspire lost its momentum in uniting its members in their chosen mission of helping the homeless. A well-planned financial strategy is helpful. Social entrepreneurs need to mix and match accessible resources and enter into creative partnerships to achieve their goals.[19]

Poor planning and preparation. Poor planning can cause problems for social enterprises. In certain cases, there is a lack of preparation for expanded demands for offered products or services.[20] Social enterprises have to carefully plan their venture growth.[21] The Canadian Society of Association Executives is a professional organization whose members include innovative firms and nonprofit organizations. In communicating with members, the firm highlights the need to build on revenue-generating products and encourages the assessment of key products that are core and relevant to the business.[22] With a keen emphasis on product winners and offerings that fit the mission, the social enterprise would more likely meet its set goals. Mike Burns, partner of business and organizational consulting firm Brody, Weiser, and Burns, indicates that business planning based on research is an anchor for success.[23]

Management issues. Social enterprises are not immune to management challenges. For instance, when hiring key executives, social enterprises are constrained to matching market rates.[24] There is currently a severe shortage of managers in the nonprofit sector that is expected to compound in the coming years. Civic Ventures has converted this obstacle into a social enterprise opportunity by recruiting baby-boomer executives as mentors and interns in nonprofit firms.[25] Some of the new recruits come from well-known firms in Silicon Valley.

Organizational issues. There are organizational barriers that need to be considered. Entrepreneurial enterprises have been observed to lack emphasis on accountability and often do not perform at an optimal level.[26] In a social entrepreneurship report, consulting firm Pepin, Tranqueda, Baker and Associates highlighted the fact that social enterprises should work on organizational challenges and barriers.[27] Organizational obstacles can exist at all levels in the company: "Social enterprises are challenged by factors such as weak boards and weak ideas."[28]

Adaptability. Some social enterprises are not as nimble as others, and they do not have the ability to pursue opportunities in a timely manner. Studies suggest that social enterprises cannot easily shift their products or services.[29] While product shifts may not be easy to accomplish, some social enterprises exhibit adaptability by staying abreast with developments and refining their competitive edge: "We constantly strive to make our processes easier."[30]

Business complexity. The nature of the work associated with social entrepreneurship is complex. Having a "double bottom line" creates added difficulties for social enterprises.[31] There are conflicting enterprise goals,[32] and several situational considerations, including labor requirements, support of the public, policies and partnerships, capital, constituency location, and relevant business incentives.[33] This business complexity takes place across different organizational levels, through diverse issues, and involves diverse protagonists.[34] Professors James Austin, Howard Stevenson, and Jane Wei-Skillern of the Harvard Business School point out the need to (a) develop a system to deal with growth opportunities; (b) thoroughly understand operational environments and market shifts; (c) work through different channels for capital access; (d) strategically network with suppliers, stakeholders, and partners; and (e) manage diverse relationships.[35] In growing their venture, Sylvan Beach, a social enterprise focused on providing life skills and employment training for "at-risk" men, constantly evolved and experimented in its quest to find a suitable operational balance. The company ended up owning several business ventures with different income streams.[36]

Limited role models and literature. Since social entrepreneurship is a fairly new field, there is a lack of knowledge on the subject. Few role models and their success formulas can be studied. Furthermore, there is limited literature on social entrepreneurship failures.[37] In recent years, it has been fortunate that social enterprises such as Endeavor have supported the writing of case studies. The developed studies have been shared with academic institutions and have helped expand understanding of the practice.

Limited government support. Lack of public policy influence can limit program success. Professors Ronnie Korosec and Evan Berman point out that lack of government support for social enterprises may be attributable to (a) control and power issues, (b) lack of clarity on the agenda, (c) lack of understanding of management competencies, (d) legal constraints, (e) conflict of interest, and (f) a focus on where funds are available rather than the real needs of the society.[38] At times, even with public policy support, little can be accomplished. Years ago, the American Association of Retired Persons, a nonprofit and nonpartisan membership group dedicated to individuals aged 50 and over, launched a triathlon series for its members. Its intention was to encourage its members to be physically active. The program, however, was short-lived; even with some public policy influence, members cannot be forced to join activities they were not interested in. Nevertheless, in most cases, government support is essential for program success. International social enterprises have worked closely with government institutions in foreign countries. Studies suggest that private initiatives alone are inadequate in addressing major social issues. Social enterprises need to engage in creative partnerships in order to achieve their goals.

Political dynamics. Politics play a role in social enterprise success. Social enterprises have to carefully select their central issues. Controversial or divisive issues, such as gun control or the right to choose, limit opportunities for finding strategic partners.[39] Finding an appropriate and timely mission opens the doors to government support. Vision Support Trading benefited from supportive government policies in the course of its business growth. YouthBuild received support from several government agencies, including the U.S. Department of Labor, the U.S. Department of Housing and Urban Development, the U.S. Department of Health and Human Services, the U.S. Department of Agriculture, and the U.S. Department of the Treasury, among others.

The outlined challenges indicate that the practice of social entrepreneurship in foreign locations is complex. There are several factors to consider, and careful planning is required. While some of the challenges are beyond a firm's control, there are aspects that can be controlled. For instance, with regard to management issues, undertaking measures to ensure that competent people are in key positions lowers the risk of blunders. Social enterprises have to carefully think through the mentioned obstacles. In working through the challenges, organizational adjustment and reinvention of approaches are necessary.

Adjustment is most essential in the internationalization process if the firm is operating in uncharted territory with a new set of barriers. In foreign locations, social enterprises are exposed to the fluctuations of market conditions.[40] Factors relating to political risks, culture, and business and economy need to be considered.

International social enterprises have to be prepared to reinvent themselves in order to cope with a new environment. For instance, a common challenge for social enterprises in the path of growth is inadequacy of support: "Social enterprises face the challenge of getting others to buy in."[41] There has been a lack of societal support for the efforts of social entrepreneurs.[42] Foreign governments may not entirely support the efforts of organizations originating from other countries. Local residents and organizations in the host country may not deem the organization's mission as relevant. International social enterprises should therefore refine their product and service offering in order to highlight the organization's value.

In the process of adjustment and reinvention, international social enterprises need to stay true to their missions. There is a need to balance operational demands in the country of origin or headquarters with new demands in foreign locations. It is often difficult to expand a social enterprise to a global scale due to the required emphasis on the primary endeavor while expansion takes place.[43] Conflicting agendas and strategic resource allocation can be serious obstacles. Inadequate financial support curtails the efficiency of expansion on social entrepreneurship activities.[44]

Aggressive adjustment and reinvention is necessary in new international locations. Organizational modifications are required due to (a) unique and evolving dynamics,[45] (b) local requirements and policies,[46] and (c) required responses to pressures pertaining to enhanced organizational control and communication.[47] A strategic fit between the organization's operational styles and the market conditions in other locations has to be measured, balanced out, and reconfigured.

International social enterprises have to engage in research and assessment to effectively manage internationalization. In the case of nongovernmental development organizations, poor analysis and organizational reflection may compromise value systems, as well as the organization's ability to carry out collaborative engagements.[48] An understanding of existing barriers is necessary. Studies point to numerous international obstacles, including (a) entry barriers;[49] (b) sociopolitical factors such as infrastructure, legal and regulatory frameworks, financial support, and social structure;[50] (c) lack of knowledge;[51] (d) scarcity of research data with which to make informed decisions;[52] and (e) operational deficiencies.[53]Additionally, when expanding overseas, firms have to consider factors such as control, costs, risk, and uncertainty.[54] Internationalization requires careful research and an understanding of the impact these factors have on the organization and its business operations.

International social enterprises need to creatively modify their organizations. For instance, one nongovernmental development organization in Brazil successfully set up an Internet-service venture in an effort to augment their revenue stream.[55] Other viable organizational adjustments and reinvention approaches for international social enterprises include (a) placing emphasis on trust and legitimacy;[56] (b) building on early credibility;[57] (c) establishing suitable networks;[58] (d) rallying for the support of the local citizenry;[59] and (e) working through possible language and cultural challenges.[60]

Conclusion

In conclusion, while there are several attractive opportunities for international social enterprises in foreign locations, challenges do exist. It is essential for international social entrepreneurs to be cognizant of these challenges and to be prepared to adapt and reinvent their organizations to cope with obstacles. The process of organizational reinvention and adjustment to a new environment requires a strong commitment and open-mindedness across all levels of the organization.

International social enterprises have to collaborate with local organizations as they carry out their missions. Lobbying for support from government organizations, academic institutions, and nongovernment organizations may bring about desirable results. Studies suggest that some governments have readjusted their visions to accommodate the greater participation of civic organizations and have encouraged the commercial implementation of projects directed at new social issues and markets.[61] Several cases on the internationalization of social enterprises point out that significant progress can be gained by collaborative engagements with the private and public sectors.

Success of social enterprises in the international arena is rarely a result of a one-time initiative. It entails a prolonged and continued effort. Constant fine-tuning and readjustment of the selected set of strategic actions is critical. Furthermore, there is a danger that although the mission is right, the venue may be wrong. Underlying conditions in a foreign country could present obstacles to venture success. In addition, the timing of the project may not be suitable, and more stringent adjustment measures will need to be implemented.

International social enterprises should be "chameleons of change." They need to constantly modify their organizations to blend with the operational terrain and evolving market conditions. The changes need to be made while staying true to the original social vision and mission.

CHAPTER 8

Make a Personal and Corporate Impact

This is our purpose: to make as meaningful as possible this life that has been bestowed upon us; to live in such a way that we may be proud of ourselves; to act in such a way that some part of us lives on.

—Oswald Spengler

Twice in his career, Philip Berber made an impact on many lives. In the 1990s, he created a company called CyBerCorp that facilitated online trading systems for investors. CyBerCorp empowered many investors and allowed them to trade for themselves. In 2000, the company was bought by the Charles Schwab Corporation for more than $450 million. Not long after, Berber built another company called Glimmer. The company supports various needs in Ethiopia. In a few short years, Glimmer has spent over $16 million for projects that resulted in the creation of 1,657 water wells, 190 schools, 99 health clinics, and 24 vet clinics. More projects are being created, and millions of lives are positively impacted. Berber believes that the success he has in international social entrepreneurship (ISE) results from revisiting the principles he has learned from his earlier business career. He has simply reapplied what he has learned in a new way. He hopes more people will follow his path.[1]

Globalization has opened a floodgate of business opportunities and challenges. Philip Berber has drawn from both opportunities and challenges to make an impact. His first business emerged as a result of financial globalization. The business enterprise he built earlier in his career centered on technological expansions and financial convergence within a globalized society. His second business, the social enterprise, addressed challenges resulting from globalization. While globalization spawned prosperity in many countries, many people in poorer nations lack the tools and resources to successfully tap into international opportunities.

Amid this landscape, Berber worked through challenges and opportunities to achieve his goals and make a positive impact on our society.

As global citizens, individuals and corporations live through the same tightly knit international landscape, yet achieve different results. The difference in success levels lies in how received information is processed in one's mind and the course of action one decides to take. For instance, in hearing about extreme poverty in Africa, some simply listen and do not care. However, there are individuals who receive the same information, process it, and are immediately motivated to act and instigate changes. These action-oriented, change instigators may soon embark on a path toward ISE. The global community offers a wide agenda for social entrepreneurs to work on. There are several pressing issues—such as poverty, AIDS, water, housing, and education—that need immediate attention.

As shown in the research and featured cases, international social entrepreneurs can make significant contributions to society. In order to make a positive personal and corporate impact, international social entrepreneurs have to consider seven developmental steps.

Assess personal and corporate citizenship. International social entrepreneurs have to engage in personal introspection. They need to understand what they are about, the real value they offer, and the contributions they can make to the world. They have to draw upon socially focused characteristics such as being visionaries, change makers, and effective communicators; being grounded in ethics and integrity; and being strategic networkers. They need to tap into diverse business-focused attributes such as being goal driven, action oriented, innovative and resourceful, financially savvy, and able to work through diversity. They have to undertake personal and corporate assessments and plan positive steps toward improvement. Through personal and organizational assessments, they take the first step toward making a personal and corporate impact in the society.

International social entrepreneurs cannot change the world on their own. An efficient team, along with a suitable organizational model, is important. A keen assessment of organizational strengths and competencies is essential. International social entrepreneurs need to gauge their levels of preparation for operating a successful social enterprise. They have to carefully evaluate their possessed social and business attributes. Socially anchored attributes include focus on potential impact on society, pursuit of change, clear vision, policy changers and transformers, commitment to stakeholders, and anchored on credibility orientation. Business-anchored attributes include market orientation, a double bottom line, an entrepreneurial angle, profit orientation, high creativity, propensity for innovation, alliance formers, sound managers, being action oriented, being well-organized, and the ability to deal with diversity. Through an understanding of organizational architecture and an understanding of what the organization can contribute, a well-conceived set of actions can be planned and implemented.

Understand the environment. International social entrepreneurs should have a good understanding of the operational environment, especially in the course of international business development. Knowledge of the factors that impact the business is helpful in crafting plans and strategies. International social entrepreneurs need to consider both challenges and opportunities. Challenges confronting social entrepreneurs are internal (within the firm) and external (outside of the firm). Internal challenges include firm attributes, management factors, process-related challenges, organization and structure, relationship and linkages, financial-related obstacles, ability to deal with risk, ethical framework, knowledge acquisition, and communication. External challenges include cultural level, social level, political factors, business and economic factors, financial landscape, and legal aspects. In striving to make an international impact, international social enterprises face countless opportunities including growth, profit, cost efficiencies, gaining of competitive advantages, performance efficiencies, and access to new knowledge and technology. Providing due consideration of these challenges and opportunities enhances the likelihood of success.

Identify the mission. With a good grasp of the market, international social entrepreneurs can pick out a suitable mission where they can make a positive personal and corporate impact. In identifying and pursuing the mission, international social entrepreneurs have to consider factors such as motivation, entrepreneurial thinking, strategy formulation, value-added components, as well as mission assessment and refinement. The proper identification and execution of the right mission sets the groundwork for future success.

Plan for internationalization. Striving to make a positive change requires looking at opportunities for contribution beyond country borders. International social entrepreneurs therefore need to define a clear path toward internationalization. Five factors need to be considered, namely, organization, technology, and knowledge; organizational relationship; management execution; and strategic direction. Organization refers to how the firm structures itself to achieve its goals and include factors such as history, firm predisposition, organizational set-up, size, management team composition, organizational diversity, and entrepreneurial disposition. Technology and knowledge pertains to the know-how of the enterprise and consists of knowledge optimization and learning, use of research and information, and use of technology. Organizational relationship deals with firm associations and includes networking ability and firm relationships. Management execution pertains to how the firm gets things done and consists of factors such as managing risk, agility, communication ability, financial competitiveness and preparedness, flexibility, and control. Strategic direction refers to courses of action implemented to achieve its goals and involves leveraging and gaining competitive edge, corporate posturing, and strategic growth and expansion. A keen understanding of the implications of these influencing factors is helpful in creating viable internationalization strategies.

Pursue strategic action. International social entrepreneurs are not just thinkers and planners—they are doers. The development and implementation of a well-defined strategic action plan is a hallmark of success. In implementing their strategies, international social entrepreneurs typically implement "inner-directed" action—that is, actions directed at the organization. Inner-directed strategies include control measures, resource utilization, financial planning, organizational enhancement, profitability, and sustainability mind-set. International social entrepreneurs also implement "outer-directed" action that responds to the external environment. There are two types of outer-directed actions: (a) proactive, consisting of factors such as niche tapping, leveraging, product positioning, growth and development, mode of entry, timing of entry, creative alliances, use of knowledge, and local resource utilization; and (b) reactive, involving navigating external influences, product customization, planning through the performance cycle, adaptation, risk management, human resource optimization, and an integrated approach. When implementing viable strategies, consideration of both inner- and outer-directed approaches is necessary.

Adjustment and reinvention. The selected sets of strategies by international social entrepreneurs require refinement as market conditions and organizational situations change. International social enterprises are confronted with numerous challenges, including poor private-sector participation, financial challenges, poor planning and preparation, management issues, organizational issues, adaptability, business complexity, limited role models and literature, limited government support, and political dynamics. International social entrepreneurs need to deftly weave through these barriers. Addressing these challenges requires preparation for organizational adjustment and reinvention. As an organization grows, international social entrepreneurs would be well served by continually measuring the impact they make and benchmarking their performance with industry norms.

Make a personal and corporate impact. Pursuing a path toward ISE situates the international social entrepreneur in a position to make significant social changes. As new challenges and opportunities are encountered, strategy refinement and cutting-edge management practices are required. International social entrepreneurs have to stay on course and remain true to their chosen mission. With globalization, every individual and corporation is in an excellent position to make a positive international impact. The path toward the successful practice of ISE is presented in Figure 8.1.

Globalization has set the stage for every citizen to make an impact and change the world. Business leaders have the ability to transform themselves into international social entrepreneurs and strive for a double and even triple bottom line. Corporate executives are poised to engage in social "intrapreneurship" and can become international social intrapreneurs by implementing social projects within their companies. Corporations can become partners, sponsors, and supporters of various social pursuits. Government and nongovernment organizations can develop innovative programs utilizing the ISE model or provide support for its growth and expansion. Educators and academic institutions can incorporate social entrepreneurship in their curriculum development and expand knowledge on the practice. Students can support and even create their own social enterprises.

Business leaders and entrepreneurs are in an excellent position to become international social entrepreneurs or to support its practice. There are at least 10 potential activities business leaders can engage in: (a) through their experience and networks, they can create a new social

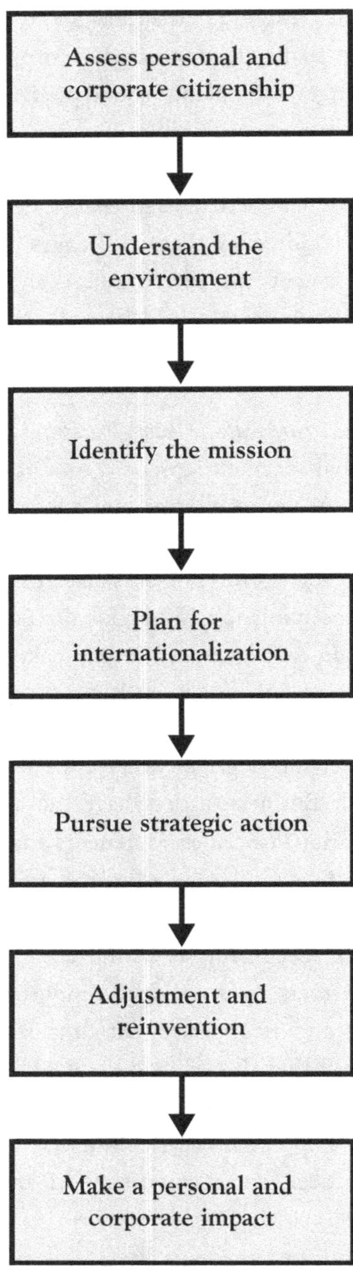

Figure 8.1. Path toward successful international social entrepreneurship.

enterprises in order to make a proactive contribution to local and international communities; (b) they can support, sponsor, collaborate, or partner with social enterprises in taking on a social issue that is of interest; (c) they can establish a socially focused division or subsidiary of their company; (d) they can acquire a social enterprise franchise and operate a venture in a foreign location where their company has a subsidiary; (e) they can integrate social enterprises in their supply chain or business operations; (f) they can offer unused property or resources and allow them to be utilized for social programs; (g) they can initiate action or support government programs that promote social enterprise activities; (h) they can partner with academe, consulting firms, and international organizations for social enterprise research and training; (i) they can form social enterprise coalitions with other companies and undertake mutually beneficial social enterprise programs; and (j) they can help expand understanding of social enterprise models by inviting social enterprise experts to speak to their organizations, civic groups, and business associations.

Private corporations and their executives are well placed to support ISE: "Corporate responsibility budgets should look to invest in socially sustainable projects and not just donate to charity."[2] There are at least 10 activities companies can pursue to support social enterprises: (a) companies can collaborate in social enterprise programs; (b) companies can offer creative forms of support and sponsorship for social enterprises (i.e., joint advertising campaigns, product donations); (c) companies can share their executive talent and provide advice to struggling social enterprises or allow them to be advisory board members of social enterprises; (d) companies can offer social enterprise training programs for their executives to expand their managerial perspective; (e) companies can explore the creation of a social enterprise division that can be a corporate spin-off or that can be operated by their retirees; (f) companies can patronize the products and services of social enterprises in their business operations; (h) companies can utilize social enterprises in selling or marketing their products in emerging markets; (i) companies can assist social enterprises in expanding into international locations where they have existing operations; (j) companies can help social enterprises by referring them to their international contacts and networks; and (k) companies can cooperate with social enterprises in joint research and information gathering in emerging markets. There are companies created primarily to support social enterprises. For instance, a company called Big Issue Invest was formed to finance top-performing social enterprises. It offers both social and financial returns to their investors. It has lent about 5 million British pounds with no default and late payments. The company has invested in social enterprises engaged in job creation, education, training, health and social care, social and financial exclusion, and environment and disability.[3]

Governments can support social entrepreneurship in many ways. Providing laws and policies that are social enterprise friendly should be helpful. Incentives and tax relief for social enterprises would stimulate social enterprise creation and attract international social entrepreneurs from foreign countries. Furthermore, providing appropriate infrastructure and systems that facilitate the growth and expansion of social enterprises could lead to a profound social impact. Providing "microcredit access for social enterprises" would be beneficial.[4] Research suggests that government programs can impact entrepreneurial activities. Efforts such as (a) market understanding and evaluation, (b) market focus, (c) identification of right support structure, (d) preparation for commercialization approaches, and (e) use of interorganizational alliances all help small ventures.[5] Furthermore, studies suggest that as firms internationalize, governments can provide support through activities such as (a) simplification of administrative procedures, (b) providing adequate information access, (c) facilitating financial resource acquisition, (d) instituting internationalization support programs, especially in the financial realm, (e) encouraging cross-institutional collaboration, and (f) providing technology, research support, and training assistance, among others.[6] Ten government policies that could contribute to the growth and expansion of social enterprises include (a) provision of tax breaks for local and international companies that engage in social entrepreneurship; (b) provision of tax breaks and incentives for companies that support social entrepreneurship; (c) including social entrepreneurship training in various government training programs; (d) offering government land or buildings at discounted rates for the development of social enterprise zones or social enterprise centers; (e) developing a specialized fund or loan facility dedicated to support social enterprises; (f) launching a nationwide informational campaign to promote social entrepreneurship and encourage participation; (g) encouraging educational institutions to include social enterprises in the curriculum; (h) undertaking and supporting social enterprise research; (i) partnering with embassies, consulting firms, and international organizations in attracting social enterprises into the country; and (j) participating in social enterprise conferences and summits. A published report by author Mark Pomerantz shows that several sectors have been participating in socially directed initiatives (see Table 8.1).

By the nature of its definition, ISE embraces diversity and aims to attract individuals from different backgrounds and sectors. The practice was defined here as *a dynamic process undertaken by individuals who are proactive, risk-taking, and mission-oriented leaders who pursue global or internationally directed initiatives that catalyze societal and policy reform,*

Table 8.1. Examples of Sector Participation in Socially Directed Initiatives

Type	Organization	Activity
Corporation	Boeing	Established the Philanthropic Work Program, which facilitates and encourages purchases from cause-oriented suppliers, such as The Lighthouse for the Blind, that manufacture sheet metal and other parts used by Boeing
Licensing firm	Nature Conservatory	Endorses and licenses brand name to companies for cause-oriented product sales and marketing
Individuals	World2Market.com (now Viatrue)	Sells Third-World products through the Internet
Foundations	Kauffman Foundation	Supports the Denali Initiative, which, in turn, provides training for directors involved in the development of social enterprises
Philanthropists	Paul Brainerd of the Aldus Corporation	Provides funding and lends expertise to environmental and socially inclined firms
Government agencies	City of Seattle	Founded the Seattle Social Investors Forum and created the Housing Trust Funds
Academic institutions	Seattle University	Collaborated with the Institute for Social Entrepreneurs in developing social entrepreneurship training programs
Community development agencies	Seattle Housing Authority	Combined housing development initiatives with the development of social programs

Source: Pomerantz (2003).

through entrepreneurial methodologies that are anchored on innovation and an adaptive spirit.

ISE is not defined by its size, business form, capital, location, or organizational structure. Rather, the practice is anchored on the dynamics of the process and on a strong desire for societal change through innovative and entrepreneurial methodologies. ISE is not solely about what one is, but rather about what one can do and become.

ISE is largely about inclusion. It is about working with groups and teams from all corners of the world as a mission is pursued: "Social enterprises are often about inclusiveness."[7] The practice highlights the need for collaboration and engagement with various stakeholders, including private corporations, governments, international organizations, sponsors, foundations, nongovernment organizations, and various constituents. Its international inclination requires embracing diversity and working with different cultures.

ISE is about global citizenship. In its practice, concerns and issues in distant corners of the world are embraced. Many international social entrepreneurs are tackling issues pertaining to poverty, health, and environmental degradation in poor nations. International social entrepreneurs conduct their affairs as active leaders in a global village.[8]

Innovative and exciting concepts are being implemented by international social entrepreneurs worldwide. Many international social entrepreneurs quietly pursue their mission in anonymity and without regard for recognition or material reward.

In essence, ISE is an attitude and a frame of mind. It emerges from a deep passion and way of living that focuses on giving rather than receiving. Not everyone is cut out to be an international social entrepreneur.

The practice of ISE requires a strong and unwavering commitment. The cases and stories featured in this book indicate that several challenges need to be addressed on both personal and organizational levels.

ISE requires a strong entrepreneurial mind-set and sound management foundation. In the course of business development, especially across international frontiers, the ability to implement action grounded in entrepreneurial methodologies can lead to success. Sound management actions enhance operational efficiencies and contribute to the achievement of the desired double or triple bottom line.

The practice of ISE is complex. Academic literature and featured cases suggest that numerous factors have to be considered in the practice of social entrepreneurship and its internationalization. In the course of internationalization, there is a need for a strong social component,[9] as well as the strategic utilization of synergies that speak to the need for attention to diverse markets, scope, and efficiencies.[10] In the course of internationalization, Professor Freek Vermeulen of the London Business School recommends that one should (a) expand where the company can optimize known knowledge, (b) transfer competitive advantage strategically, whether through greenfield investment or acquisition, (c) prepare to customize approaches to suit markets, and (d) assimilate quickly, then move on to other opportunities.[11]

Success in the practice of ISE lies in the organization's ability to manage opportunities and challenges. Based on gathered research, Table 8.2 highlights opportunities and challenges that affect international social enterprises.

Table 8.2. Opportunities and Challenges Affecting International Social Enterprises

Opportunities	Challenges
Global environment to ease the flow of idea transfers and cross-border communication	Lack of societal support
Convenience in the formulation of cross-cultural collaborations and partnerships	Need for a balanced and strategic expansion
Increased incidences of social enterprise success	Capital and appropriate resources
Empowerment to make social enhancement and economic impact in foreign communities	Flexibility and adaptability
Wide-open area for the creative and innovative utilization of social entrepreneurship approaches	Need for locational awareness (i.e., sociocultural, legal, political, social, business, economic)
Evolving dynamics of structures and systems	Need to strengthen communication and international coordination
New modalities for the practice of entrepreneurial skills and international business enhancements	Inconsistency in government support
	Disparity in operational frameworks in international locations
	Infrastructure issues
	Establishment of trust and legitimacy
	Creation of a dynamic and effective support network
	Language and cultural barriers

The information featured in Table 8.2 highlights the various factors that affect the practice of ISE. Gathered literature emphasizes the need for the organization to prepare to deal with such complexity.[12]

The challenges confronting international social enterprises may or may not be within the firm's control. Table 8.3 lists the types of challenges and their controllability.

In Table 8.3, uncontrollable and partially uncontrollable factors refer to challenges that exist in foreign locations that can obstruct the operational efficiency of the international social enterprise. As shown in the table, these challenges are not entirely within the control of the firm; however, the challenges remain manageable to a certain extent. For instance, a firm can take action to respond to the following challenges: (a) lack of societal support can be managed by the clear articulation of the issues to relevant and influencing parties; (b) financial challenges can be addressed by embarking on an aggressive international financial campaign; (c) inconsistency in government support can be managed through a policy reform campaign and the involvement of the government in project implementation; (d) disparity in operational frameworks can be fixed by the utilization of management adaptation and flexibility; and (e) challenge in infrastructure can be resolved through innovation and the application of creative practices. Though these challenges inhibit operational efficiencies, all remain relatively manageable.

The controllable and partially controllable factors included in Table 8.3 refer to challenges that an international social enterprise faces that

Table 8.3. Controllable and Uncontrollable Challenges Affecting International Social Enterprises

Uncontrollable/ Partially Uncontrollable	Controllable/ Partially Controllable
Lack of societal support	Balanced and strategic expansion
Access to capital	Flexibility and adaptability
Inconsistency in government support	Location awareness
Disparity in operational framework	Strengthen communication and international communication
Infrastructure issues	Establishment of trust and legitimacy
	Creation of dynamic and effective support network
	Language and cultural barriers

are directly within its control. The firm is in the position to manage these challenges by implementing measures such as (a) balanced and coordinated international expansion, (b) flexibility of structure and management, (c) research of the new environment, (d) enhancing cross-border communication and activity coordination, (e) providing attention to credibility building, (f) building an effective support network, and (g) preparing and training organizational members for language and cultural misunderstandings. By taking proactive action on factors they can control, social enterprises are in a better position to succeed in foreign locations.

It is evident that these influencing factors require the creation of efficient organizational models. The created models need to respond to internal and external organizational challenges and expand opportunities.

While management of operational challenges is important for an international social enterprise, even more daunting is finding the balance between achieving its social goals and attaining profitability.[13] Finding the operational model that addresses dual or triple goals is an intense challenge, especially since markets and organizations evolve.

From the gathered research, it is evident that practice of ISE stands to benefit from sound management approaches by a committed management team. The following agenda, comprised of twelve approaches, is highly recommended for international social entrepreneurs.

Formulation of a clear international vision. International social entrepreneurs need to have a clear and coherent mind-set when expanding their organizations across international frontiers. Effective implementation of strategies becomes possible with a clear vision.[14] With a well-focused and united organization, resource utilization may be optimized.

Objective assessment of firm's strength and weaknesses. The assessment and understanding of firm competencies are important considerations as international social entrepreneurs expand their mission into foreign locations. Small firms tend to integrate and expand their marketing and entrepreneurship practices as they start to internationalize.[15] A firm's key competencies may have high value overseas, and venture internationalization could be convenient.

Knowledge of the new environment(s). In implementing socially directed programs in new environments, international social entrepreneurs need to fully understand the intrinsic causes of the issues, the dynamics of the location (sociocultural, political, legal, infrastructure, business, and economic), and the availability of support networks. Thorough research and keen understanding of the new location will aid in the planning of effective business development approaches and will provide insights on the management of challenges and location barriers. There is benefit accrued to understanding the market and the sociocultural dynamics of a new location.[16]

Selective leveraging of social issues. There is merit in the practice of social leveraging, or transferring the management of social issues in one location to another venue, where it is needed or desired. In pursuing this strategy, international social entrepreneurs have to be observant of the parallelisms and differences that exist between the home environment and the target locations. Though social issues in international locations may be the same, the root causes may differ, therefore requiring adjustments in the implementation modes. Furthermore, if a social enterprise aims to address several international social issues, focusing on the most relevant and most applicable in the target location would likely yield better results.

Focus on niche locations. International social entrepreneurs may face limited growth prospects due to constraints in time and resources. There is value in focusing on niche locations where more significant impacts may be made. Research suggests that small firms gain an advantage by operating in niche markets utilizing a unique portfolio of competencies.[17]

Well-planned international expansion. As social issues span the globe, a viable internationalization approach for international social entrepreneurs would be to prioritize projects according to locations that are closely aligned with the firm's competencies or where help is most needed: "Global social entrepreneurship is not just about charitable giving, it's about making a real difference over a sustained period of time."[18]

Effective strategy. Strategic planning is an important consideration for international social entrepreneurs. Thinking through financial aspects in the growth process is important.[19] Poor international performance has been attributed to lack of planning, haphazard implementation, and inadequate risk assessment.[20] There is a need to consider the interplay of factors relating to degree of control, costs, and risks in international entry.[21] There is merit in fully understanding the social value proposition (SVP), where social entrepreneurship strategy is designed with high consideration for people, opportunity, and capital, as well as influencing tax, regulatory, sociocultural, demographic, political, and macroeconomic factors.[22]

Strong network and credibility. Once an appropriate location is determined, international social entrepreneurs need to build a strong presence in the new environment. There are merits associated with gathering efficient support networks[23] and the building of credibility.[24] Strategic partnership is key, as illustrated by the Global Resolve Project in Ghana by the Arizona State University. Collaboration through networking and joint project management can be beneficial.[25]

Urgency and issue awareness. Elevating the social cause to a level of crisis and urgency facilitates the gathering of early support. Positioning the social issue in a level of crisis increases its relevance.[26] This approach may help address complacency in societal and government support in foreign locations. In social entrepreneurship initiatives, government support through generation awareness, facilitation of resource access, and program collaboration can be very helpful.[27] Governments can provide funds and incentives[28] and increase awareness of critical issues.[29]

Dynamic and motivated team. As in any business enterprise, the international social entrepreneur's ability to recruit an action-oriented team leads to remarkable results. A team's sharing of values and commitment to the enterprise can facilitate and expedite the implementation of the organization's agenda. Author Kris Herbst interviewed social entrepreneurs Aleta Margolis, Amy Barzach, David Erickson, Kevin Long, Matthew Johnson, and Van Jones to identify viable field approaches for practitioners. The responses of these individuals pointed out the following factors associated with social entrepreneurship: (a) there is a need to precisely identify and understand one's social passion; (b) formulation of a vision is essential; (c) success is anchored on a practitioner's ability to gather support from effective teams, mentors, allies, and strategic partners; (d) a collaborative environment needs to be nurtured; (e) flexibility and openness to the experience of others is crucial; (f) a proactive attitude brings results; and (g) focus should be in areas where the most significant impact can be made.[30]

Sound business management practices. International social entrepreneurs need to be on the lookout for the best management practices. Useful methods to consider include the following: (a) emphasis on revenue generation without losing focus on organizational mission,[31] (b) attention to value creation and strategic management and decision making,[32] (c) establishment of performance measures, awareness generation, training and development, and collaborative engagements,[33] and (d) giving importance to financial issues due to its impact on the achievement of the planned mission.[34] In addition, management adjustments are required in response to the local culture, governance, laws, business and economic environment, and infrastructure.

Continuous innovation. The international business environment is constantly evolving. There are pressures for the enhancement of service deliveries,[35] and there is continuous emergence of new systems and practices.[36] International social entrepreneurs have to continually explore new avenues for enhancing service deliveries in international locations, and must plan strategic responses in a timely and efficient manner. The future success of international social entrepreneurs is grounded in the efficiency of networks, alliances, and creative use of technologies.[37]

This action agenda is a viable tool for international social entrepreneurs, and can serve as an instrument for the success of international endeavors. Furthermore, Professors Paul Bloom and Aaron Chatterji recommend the use of an organizational model called SCALERS—or, Staffing, Communicating, Alliance building, Lobbying, Earnings generation, Replicating, and Stimulating market forces as a combination of actions suitable for the expansion of social enterprises.[38] For instance, if one intends to expand a social enterprise in an emerging market, the SCALERS model would lead one to ask the following pertinent questions:

1. How will I staff the operations while ensuring quality service delivery? How will my staffing impact my other operations and overall bottom line?
2. How do I communicate my message effectively to the various stakeholders? What needs to be communicated clearly?
3. What alliances should I be building on? Which ones should I give priority to?
4. What lobbying would need to be done? How will it be done most effectively?
5. How will this expansion impact my profitability? What are the costs and revenue opportunities? When do I get a return on my investment?

6. How will I replicate the business model to capture advantages relating to scale and scope? Which geographical areas and market segments should be prioritized?

7. How will I shape the market? What will my overall contribution be?

International social enterprises, private corporations, government institutions, and other organizations engaging in social initiatives would benefit from specialized training: "Corporations should support training and education for social entrepreneurship."[39] Mentoring and coaching have proven to be helpful for social entrepreneurs.[40] Entrepreneurial training is best anchored on experiential learning.[41] Oftentimes, actual creation of venture plans opens the door toward practice-oriented learning.[42] Diverse approaches suit entrepreneurial training; however, an emphasis on clear conceptual frameworks that allow learners to experience and solve different pieces of the puzzle can make a significant impact on learning.[43] In the case of the McGuire Center at the University of Arizona, entrepreneurial training places an emphasis on topics such as sales forecasting, cost determination, and financial statement preparation.[44] Professors Paul Tracey and Nelson Phillips propose six steps for social enterprise training: (a) integrate issues that tap into the experience and interests of participants, (b) gather the viewpoints of experienced practitioners and field experts through guest visits, (c) provide participants the opportunity to learn by creating teaching cases, (d) have participants develop a social enterprise plan, (e) facilitate experiential learning through consulting projects, and (f) facilitate participation in internships.[45] For entrepreneurship trainers, Professors Matthew Mars and Sharon Garrison suggest the following: (a) keep an open mind when receiving out-of-the-box student proposals or ideas; (b) prepare to collaborate, communicate, and interact with several groups; (c) try applying theories in new and creative ways; and (d) support ideas through high enthusiasm.[46] Academic institutions may find value in initiating or expanding social enterprise programs. A study in the United Kingdom uncovered that younger people tend to be interested in social entrepreneurship.[47] Students tend to be supportive of social endeavors. More than 900 students from Stanford University supported a 24-hour dance marathon and successfully raised $150,000 for Partners in Health: "There is a need to excite and engage the youth in social entrepreneurship."[48]

Aside from academic institutions, businessmen, private corporations, and government institutions should take more aggressive measures in the social enterprise movement. On a personal level, "we should all be passionate about a cause, and start caring about issues beyond ourselves."[49] On a corporate or organizational level, "we all need to roll up our sleeves and get our hands dirty."[50] According to Billy Shore, chairman of Community Wealth Ventures, "There is a need for community wealth building and its creation depends on combining the talents of businesses and non-profits."[51]

Globalization has brought the world closer together. With heightened integration, it has become far easier to see the good, the bad, and the ugly aspects of society. New technologies have transformed business modalities and the speed of cross-border implementation. With the growing number of international social entrepreneurs in our midst, there is reason for optimism. In our global village, new leaders that seek meaningful contributions will continue to emerge. These individuals shall transform the world in creative ways and will make deep and lasting personal and corporate impacts.

APPENDIX

Tale of the Globalist

There is a loftier ambition than merely to stand high in the world. It is to stoop down and lift mankind a little higher.

—Henry Van Dyke

A Beach Resort in Bali, Indonesia, July 8, 2010, 10:00 p.m.

They were crouched together by a campfire along the beach. The waves splashed violently as the firewood cracked in the fire. No one stirred or made a sound; they were too absorbed at the moment.

Finally, John Donner, the American organizer spoke. "Thank you for being here, you will find what I have to say interesting.' The six others at the campfire listened intently to the 28-year-old multimillionaire. He had a reputation as a man of few words and as a master of time management. After all, as a tech-savvy entrepreneur, he built a global e-commerce empire in just 2 years.

Elena Chavez smiled. "By the way, congratulations, John. I heard your company was listed in the top-10 fastest growing firms for the second year in a row."

Donner smiled shyly. "Thank you. You're not doing too bad yourself. Your fashion magazine and clothing lines are hot topics in New York. How's your father?"

"Still a busy government official in Brazil. I was there for a fashion shoot just 2 weeks ago."

"Why so short a notice for this meeting, John?" asked Jack Wang. A college buddy of John Donner at the University of California at Los Angeles, Jack has been a supplier to several of John's businesses. In addition, his family owns large commercial properties in Hong Kong and China.

"Everyone else had ample preparation time, Jack. Since you live in Hong Kong, I figured the trip to Bali wouldn't be so inconvenient. Also, I've known you to respond very well under pressure."

Steve Blake, the Australia-based real estate and entertainment tycoon sipped on his beer and muttered, "What are you complaining about, Jack? You took a flight to get here; I sailed. Got to live life a bit more, mate."

James Edwards, the Englishman, stood up and stepped closer to Sabrina Lopez, a voluptuous Filipina. He sat behind her and massaged her back. "If you ask me, I'm happy enough to be in this lovely beach with gorgeous Sabrina. How have you been my dear?"

"Been great, James. Thank you. My venture capital fund has quadrupled over the past 2 years, and investments in emerging markets have paid off handsomely." She smiled, enjoying the back rub. "How's your management consulting company?"

"Couldn't be better. Just collected 10 million pounds from a client last week. You should take a closer look at a new merger I'm planning—could be a worthwhile investment."

"No, thank you, James. I'm a little bothered by your reputation." Sabrina smiled sweetly.

"What reputation? I'm just a lowly businessman trying to earn a living." Everybody around the campfire smiled knowingly. Recent news articles have exposed his involvement in shady deals relating to arms smuggling and money laundering. Highly intelligent and legally savvy, James loved to pursue business transactions that tested the boundaries of international law. He is reputed to have earned over $100 million in questionable international deals in recent years. Intriguingly, he had the uncanny ability to remain legally unscathed.

"You should consider donating some of your corporate earnings to my research fund in South Africa, James. We've already helped thousands of locals and may take the medical product internationally," Dr. Pete Omalu suggested. "We could certainly use your talents in creative international product distribution." Dr. Omalu has been at the forefront of medical research in Africa—his biotechnology company pioneered innovative herbal treatments for a wide range of ailments. His combined passion for science and philanthropy has contributed to his popularity and success in the region.

John Donner stood beside the blazing fire and looked intently at each of his colleagues seated around the campfire.

He started, "Again, thank you all for coming. I have met each of you in various international settings and occasions. I'm glad to see that the rest of you had the chance to get to know each other a little better prior to our meeting tonight."

John paused and inched closer to the group. "As you may have observed, everyone gathered here tonight is a multimillionaire. You are all tested and proven international achievers under the age of 40. Aside from being wealthy, you are all reputable think tanks in your industry and movers in your geographic location. Forgive me for the intrusion, but I have also done a thorough background check on each of you. It might be better that I come clean now. I am aware that all of us gathered here tonight have yet to live our life's fullest potential. We have proven ourselves to be winners in the international financial arena yet have nothing to show in the area of social contribution. We've all made money at a young age but have yet to make a real difference in the global society. Like me, you are all starting to get bored and are perhaps seeking an even greater challenge in life. Am I correct?"

John looked around the campfire for affirmation. There was not a single dissent. This is good, he thought, actually better than expected. An interruption may have destroyed his thought flow and momentum.

"If there's anyone here tonight who is not willing to commit one full year in order to pursue a life changing challenge, please feel free to leave. There would be no hurt feelings if you decide to leave now. I will reimburse you for all your expenses. If you decide to stay, you shall be bound to participate in a secret global game. I cannot disclose anything other than the fact that this game would likely change your life and lead you to face perhaps the greatest mental and physical challenge in your career. While doing so, you may even save a few souls. Anyone backing out?"

No one moved or said anything. John paused and stared at each person around the campfire. After a few minutes, he began, "Very well then, as anticipated—you are all players. Here's the game. I am challenging each of you to a game we'll secretly call 'The Globalist.' The object of this match is to identify who, among us, could make the greatest positive impact in our world in the span of 1 year. There shall be seven of us competing, and I believe all are tough and worthy opponents. With full commitment and the appropriate mix of strategies, all of us seated around this campfire tonight have the ability to make a significant international impact. This competition, however, is not about making an impact—it's about making that greatest singular global impact. In exactly a year, we'll all meet here again and vote on the winner—the person in this select group who has made the greatest contribution to the world. The winner shall be bestowed the secret title 'The Globalist.'"

Dr. Omalu spoke, "This sounds intriguing. But, what are the rules?"

John nodded, "Before the rules, there is one other thing. Like all games, the motivating factor must be clear. This game is not only about winning. It's also about the avoidance of losing. In order to make the game even more exciting, and ensuring everyone's commitment, I am proposing a financial component to the game. Each of us would put in $1 million as money in the pot. Winner takes all."

Steve Blake, the Australian, laughed. "Are you kidding? The total pot money wouldn't excite my secretary—I would suggest $3 million each."

James Edwards was quick to the draw. "Five million dollars each—for a total pot money of $35 million and the title 'The Globalist.' Plus huge publicity in international magazines."

"In addition," Jack Wang countered, "losing competitors would provide full support to the winner in various forms of media, and personally nominate 'The Globalist' for awards and recognition, such as the Nobel Peace Prize and the Global Leader for Tomorrow Award given by the World Economic Forum."

Sabrina Lopez exclaimed, "Now I'm really motivated!"

"I would really hate to lose. But, admittedly this game is a thrill," said Elena Chavez.

John Donner stepped in, "Okay, looks like we're all getting excited. The pot money of $35 million, plus publicity, plus international awards and recognition. Not bad for a year's work. There are just three rules: (1) no two participants can work with each other or communicate with each other within a period of one year, (2) there are no limits to capitalization you put in your planned project, and (3) the project should positively impact the lives of at least 1 million people worldwide at the end of 1 year. We shall meet here again on the same day and at same time next year to vote on the winner. The clock starts ticking at midnight. Any questions?"

"What if there's a tie after we vote? Can we have two winners?" Elena Chavez asked.

John cut in quickly, "There can only be one Globalist. We'll worry about the voting mechanics during the voting night. What is most important is that we select the winner who has made an impact on the greatest number of lives. Are we all in? This game is strictly confidential; not even our family members should know about it. This challenge, and everything we discussed, stays within the confines of this campfire. After we depart, I shall put out the fire and we shall no longer talk about it—until it is again relit at the same time next year. Violation of this secrecy is grounds for disqualification and forfeiture of your contribution to the pot."

"John's right," Jack interrupted. "If others get hold of this, our real motives become questionable and it can stain our reputation. A media frenzy can also be disastrous."

"Also, wouldn't there be legal complications arising from the $35 million pot money?" Elena Chavez asked.

"Not really, it can be treated as a personal donation," Sabrina Lopez replied.

"The winner can deposit the pot money in a Swiss account. I'll help take care of it; this is my specialization, after all," added James Edwards.

"It's all set then—our vow of utmost secrecy," John Donner said. "Before you leave don't forget to leave your $5 million check with my secretary Lori. She'll hold the check for us and will keep it in a secret bank vault. You'll find her beside the concierge desk at 8:00 a.m. sharp tomorrow. She will remain there until all of us have left the resort. There will be no further communication between us. I'll see you on July 8 next year, 10 p.m., at this very same campfire. Good luck to all; may the best man or woman win!"

Everyone rose and parted.

John Donner: Peace Through Technology

John Donner was very pensive in his limousine ride to the airport. He had mixed emotions. A part of his psyche was pleased at the thought of competing with the best minds in the world to make a positive international impact. His darker side was plagued with fear. It is not at all funny to lose $5 million. He had imagined that the team would have found a million-dollar bet to be acceptable. A $5 million gambit was way on the high side.

The hell with it, he thought to himself. *I've won many times in my career, conquered insurmountable challenges, dealt with the toughest business competitors. I can win this game.* He basked at the thought of $35 million and the possibility of a Nobel Peace Prize nomination. Ahhh . . . the trappings of wealth and fame. What more can a man ask for?

He was in his New York office the following day. Sitting by his large mahogany desk, he felt the usual feel of elegance. The office was well decorated with antiques and memorabilia of his international exploits. It was a far cry from the Spartan and exotic resort in Bali. Bali seemed like a distant memory, thousands of miles away, yet it evoked the same nagging thoughts.

How can I make the most significant international impact? One that would be far greater than my competitors?

He tore out a piece of his corporate stationary and scribbled the following words:

1. Greatest international impact
2. Technology based
3. Affecting at least 1 million people
4. Sustainable
5. Personal project capitalization: $5 million

He dialed an office number. "Jeff Goldman, please." He did not have to wait long.

"Jeff, this is John. I need you to put $5 million in a reserve fund for me. Need it for an investment in a tech project . . . No, I don't have the project specifics yet. Don't argue with me, I need this . . . When? I'll take the money in stages then, with the first million in 3 weeks. The rest I can take in the intervals of 1 month? . . . No, make it 3 weeks. . . . Jeff, spare me the details. Just get it done, okay?"

His mind raced. Yes, technology. Technology shapes the world. It enhances one's ability to make an impact across borders in the fastest manner possible. Surely there's something out there that could impact the lives of a million people, maybe even tens of millions, perhaps a hundred million. He smiled at the prospect. But what could it be?

Key word: arbitrage. He could acquire new technologies from electronic hotbeds across the United States and facilitate their transfer to emerging locations where they are most needed. Technology transfers and the Internet can liberate people in countries in the Middle East—countries like Iraq or Afghanistan. Technology can help boost their competitiveness within the global landscape. It heightens the productivity of people, stimulates business activity, and leads to the creation of jobs. Ultimately, millions will benefit. Should he pick one country in particular? A combination of countries? Perhaps the entire region?

Bingo! The Middle East, he thought. The region has millions of poor and deprived people, unable to efficiently compete in the global environment due to the lack of technological access. Yes, he could make a wide range of technologies, products, and services affordable and accessible to the masses in the region. Though the project is specifically targeted at only one region in the world, its implications for international peace and stability span the globe.

Fantastic. He'll need to build a new company for this, say—Gulf Peace Technologies (GPT). Technological property rights, computer hardware, and software from U.S. firms can be pooled together by GPT and brought in to the Middle East in phases. He could even create a Technological Peace Corps, which can provide a cadre of volunteers to work in the region. This project will not only help millions, it will create and nurture a positive image of America.

John Donner was very excited. He couldn't wait to get started. He planned to form a parent organization that can spearhead the project. It can be called the Gulf Peace Foundation. He can lobby support from the U.S. government for supplementary funding.

Yes, and corporate sponsorships, too. He could get support from Microsoft, Hewlett Packard, Dell, and all the other large technological players. It can be done, he thought. It can snowball to become something even bigger. Millions will benefit.

In the following days, he gathered his executive team and planned out the project. Together they broke out the major tasks and the timelines:

1. Creation of the Gulf Peace Foundation—1 month
2. Formulation of the organizational mission, vision, handbook, and website—2 months

3. Formation of an alliance with the Peace Corps—2 months
4. Sponsorship from the major U.S. technological players—3 months
5. Creating and training the Gulf Peace technological corps—3 to 5 months
6. Gather support from the U.S. government—3 to 5 months
7. Active media and publicity campaign for the project—3 to 5 months
8. Setting up and activation of the Gulf Peace technological centers in key locations across the Middle East—6 to 8 months
9. Project implementation, monitoring, and assessment—7 to 10 months
10. Project evaluation and assessment of impact—10 to 11 months

The budget of $5 million seemed adequate. Support from the major technological players seemed plausible considering that the companies would likely want to build goodwill in the region as they expand their markets. Support from the U.S. government appears to be a reasonable expectation. John Donner planned on immersing himself in the project, work doubly hard, and creatively use his networks in the private industry and government. The timing was extremely tight, but he was well positioned to steamroll the project. A couple of calls to government officials in Washington, DC, confirmed his favorable expectations.

The plan looked superb. He jumped into action.

Jack Wang: International Safety Net

Jack Wang peered through the glass window of his 10th-floor suite in Hong Kong. He stared at the droves of people rushing to work. He thought about the millions of people way below him, working in 9-to-5 jobs, yet barely managing to survive. A tinge of pity engulfed him. He wondered how many in this herd of humanity had the opportunity to actually have three decent meals a day, despite such a hectic lifestyle.

He shifted his eyes to a group construction workers situated on a tall building across from his. A man was walking through a thin steel frame, carefully doing a balancing act. Certainly, this was a high-risk and low-yield proposition, payable with one's life. The irony of it, he thought, all the technology in the hands of humanity, the ability to launch space shuttles way beyond Earth, yet little can be done to protect the life of a construction worker hundreds of feet above the ground. He shook his head at the incongruence of wealth and technology that exist in our modern society.

It was now 8:30 a.m., as he looked at his watch. Time to leave for the weekly 9:00 a.m. breakfast meeting with his brother Arthur. He decided to walk to the Renaissance Harbour View Hotel.

He found Arthur seated in a corner table, browsing a newspaper. He pulled up a side chair and requested coffee.

Arthur folded the paper, looked up, and complained, "When are these stocks ever going to get in shape again?"

Jack smiled, "Probably never, Art. What's the big deal? You have enough money to last you and your family 10 lifetimes."

"Are you kidding?" Arthur countered. "Nothing is totally safe in this new economy. People's fortunes can get wiped out in an instant. Remember the Asian crisis? Then, the global meltdown? We're all living on a tightrope, chum."

Jack also remembered the construction worker he saw earlier. "Yes, perhaps some people are walking in a far thinner rope than others."

"Am I sensing some sentimentalism, or am I just hungry? Let's go get some buffet."

With plates filled, the brothers started breakfast.

"I'm thinking of pursuing a social project, Art," Jack said slowly.

"What type of social project? You're not thinking about getting into politics are you?"

"No, not politics. Just a pure civic project."

"Why not join the Rotary Club or the Lions Club? You've had several invitations in the past."

"I'm thinking of a large-scale, socially oriented initiative."

Arthur stopped eating and stared at his brother for awhile, "Such as . . . ?"

"I haven't decided yet. But it should be something that would positively impact the lives of many in Southeast Asia—maybe the Asia–Pacific region—I don't really know yet."

"Is it going to be a money earner?" Arthur asked.

"Probably not, but it would need to be sustainable."

"I don't really believe you. How can you find time for this project? You hardly even have time for your family, chum!"

"Well, I've decided to devote one full year to humanity. What's our average lifespan now, 70 years? Why can't anyone give at least 1 year of their lives to their fellow men?"

"What others do, Jack, is cut up their contribution to society into minutes, hours, days, over several years. Do something good one step at a time, without disrupting their lives. It's more sensible and more of the norm."

"Precisely," Jack added. "That's why there is so little social impact taking place in our world today. Social causes always take the back seat and are barely considered alongside life's so-called priorities. What people need to do is really set their sight on something of utmost significance and give it full and exclusive attention."

"Yeah, right—aren't families and careers of great significance?" Arthur argued.

"True, but if you live for 70 years, devote 69 years to a career and your family, and a mere 1 year to a cause, aren't you still giving more to what is significant to you? I'm not suggesting that one should let go of responsibilities or priorities, but rather just modify the approach in order to make a greater contribution and impact."

"I see what you mean, but how sure are you that taking one full year is better?" Arthur asked.

"We only make a small dent in our society if we strive to pursue several activities simultaneously—we can make a bigger social impact if we focus on just one. It's like introducing a new real estate project to the market. Didn't we achieve more success when we marketed properties one at a time? Wasn't our achievement bigger and faster when we stayed focused and concentrated our attention exclusively on that one single property development? It's the same principle. You know the drill."

"So what is that big social market you want to look at?"

"That's what I wanted to talk to you about. Who do you think are the most deprived and the least-served segments in Asian society?"

"There are several, Jack," Arthur said flatly.

"I know, but which segment do you think needs the most attention?"

"Why ask me, chum? You know I'm a full-blooded businessman. Social responsibility happens to be at the bottom of my list."

"You've traveled more extensively around Asia in your quest for profit; I figured you've seen a lot more depressing sites than I have."

"True." Arthur sat still for a moment and again mumbled, "Quite true." He was absorbed in his own thoughts.

Arthur slowly pushed his plate away and took a slow sip of orange juice. He looked at his brother with a pained and sad look. He took out a cigar and said softly, "I'll tell you a story."

He started to light his cigar and offered another one to Jack. They lit their cigars together.

"I once met a man in a small town in the southern part of China," Arthur started. "He was a very nice fellow with five children. He worked at a mining firm that I bought minerals from. He actually drove me around town and to the big cities. Lee, his name, even took me to his small house. A depressing sight, actually—an 8-square-meter wooden hut, where the entire family lived. I remember thinking that day that Lee's house was worse than a jail cell. But, nevertheless, the poor family appeared happy. I liked Lee and asked for him every time I traveled to the mining firm. About a year ago, I learned that Lee had an accident at the mining site. His body was crushed and he lost both legs and an arm. Worse, his firm didn't have accident insurance for workers. Lee's wife did not have commercial skills; as a result, their five children were sent to different orphanages across China. Think of it, in one twist of fate, a man lost his limbs and his entire family with them. And nobody can do a darn thing about it."

"Where's Lee now?" Jack asked sadly.

"Last I heard, he was begging in the streets of his small town. The sad thing about today's society is that in many countries, there are no safety nets for the losers or those who are out on luck." There was a trace of anguish and anger in Arthur's voice.

Jack sat quietly; the story stirred his soul. Arthur's story meant something more to both men—their father was crippled in a vehicular accident 2 decades ago. They are all too familiar with the pain and trauma of debilitation to both the victim and the family. Jack wondered how many out there shared Lee's story. And how many more are lined up to face a similar fate?

"Isn't accident insurance mandatory for companies?" Jack asked in a displeased manner.

"Not in several small companies located around the world, especially in Asia and Africa," Arthur countered.

"Maybe that should be my social project. An international accident insurance fund that will provide a safety net for millions of poor people worldwide."

"Part of the reason why people don't have them, chum, is that they can't afford to pay them with their meager wages. And, they don't have access to information about these insurance policies."

"What if there was an accident insurance fund where workers contribute $1 a month, and it pays $10,000 for any accident—would this have helped Lee? Might he have been able to afford it?"

"I guess it's a yes on both counts. He could have afforded to pay $1 a month if he fully understood the benefits. Ten thousand dollars in that small town would have gotten Lee a long way. If he kept that money in his town's bank, the interest alone would have fed him and his family for a long time."

Jack was suddenly excited. "Does that mining firm have Internet access?"

"Why do you ask?" Arthur wondered.

"If I develop a website as the primary medium for information dissemination, payment, and delivery, it could spread out faster, be accessible to millions, and it would help me keep the operating cost down. What makes insurance expensive is the high operating costs associated in operating the venture. If I eliminate the high administrative costs and focus on the high-yield investment returns for the dollar, I might make it fly."

"It sounds interesting. Internet access is spreading rapidly. How many people do you think you'll reach?" Arthur asked.

"With a dollar a month as payment? Maybe millions. The project can be a hybrid of an insurance company and a foundation. I might have to align myself with the World Bank or a top-tier financial development institution."

"How long before you'll ever get this project started? What makes you so sure that the banks, companies, and governments will cooperate?"

"I plan to get this project going in 2 to 3 months. It would be nice to have the support of governments, but it is not critical to the success of the project. Besides, I will be dealing primarily with companies and individuals, right? We are living in global society that is essentially borderless. A floodgate of ideas and capital flow freely across countries. Hasn't the financial world been liberated for some time now?"

Arthur smiled and stubbed his cigar in the ashtray. He hasn't seen his younger brother this excited in a while. He was amused to see the altruistic side of Jack. He has known his brother to be a doer and achiever in the business frontier, but Jack has never shown earlier interest in social work. He looked at his brother and smiled; Jack would certainly make progress in this project. His global network can make the world spin.

"So, how much resources are you putting in for this project?" Arthur asked.

"Anywhere between $5 and 10 million is my initial guess. I'll need a lot of help to get the word out fast. I plan to recruit at least 1 million poor people into the program within a year."

"What's the rush?"

Jack smiled inwardly. "Art, I'm giving 1 year of my life full time for this project. Might as well make a huge impact." Thoughts pertaining to the $35 million pot money, the potential fame and recognition, and the spread of international goodwill flashed in his mind. Winning "The Globalist" game seems within reach. He wondered what the other six competitors were up to. He was exuberant. "So, what help can I expect from my brother in this project?"

It was Arthur's turn to smile. "What about $5 million and 2 months of my time, chopped up into hours, minutes, and days?"

"Deal." Jack said. They shook hands, signed the bill, and left.

Back in his office, Jack plotted out his agenda and timeframes. He could get the insurance firm running with an active website in 3 months at the latest. He will have 9 months to gather at least 1 million documented insurance beneficiaries. This was not going to be easy. Then, a thought struck him. If the average Asian family consisted of four members, wouldn't other family members be counted as recipients of good will as well? Meaning, if he successfully recruits only 300,000 into the program, it would positively impact the lives of over a million people as a result of the protection and safety net that they receive as a family? If he gets half a million people into the program, essentially, he helps around 2 million. The figure was well above the target. Time was of the essence. But the project was doable; more importantly, it was measurable. He would have all the names listed in a computer database. What better evidence can he show the other competitors?

Jack Wang was a shrewd investor, and he knew a lot of investment gurus. He was confident he could turn those $1 monthly contributions into thousands of dollars in a matter of years.

What a difference a day has made. He had a lighthearted feeling like he never had before. He was glad he had breakfast with his brother.

Jack stood up from his desk to look out of the window again. The construction worker was still working on the tall building across from him. "Hang on, I'll take care of you, buddy," he muttered.

He pressed the office intercom. "Sofie, can you ask the Special Projects Committee to report to my office? Yes, right now. Thank you." It was time to get the Asian Charity and Insurance Fund rolling.

Steve Blake: Breakfast Across Borders

Steve Blake stared at the stars in the sky. He was sipping champagne on his yacht, the *Sydney Belle*. Gorgeous night, he thought; all he lacked was company. He always knew life at the top was lonely, but he didn't realize it was this lonely.

Born to relatively poor Australian parents, his sickly father was an alcoholic, while his mother was a determined woman who worked hard to keep the family's small farm.

Poverty and growing up in a remote hometown did not stop young Blake from conquering Australia and New Zealand in a big way. After leaving the farm at 16, he prowled the streets of Sydney to make a quick buck here and there. He eventually saw an opportunity in the entertainment industry, managing undiscovered prime talents and selling them to entertainment networks. Soon after, he became the entertainment industry master and guru. The bars and entertainment networks followed. In the past 3 years, his ownership stake in casinos, cruise lines, and various hotel properties brought in millions.

His only regret in life was never having a wholesome and happy family life. Three divorces and four children later, he felt truly alienated. He hardly knew his children anymore, more so, his ex-wives.

It was a mighty steep price to pay for a glorious career.

The calm night opened a floodgate of life memories. "It's good to have moments like this," he thought. He hardly ever had time for introspection in hectic Sydney. He was glad John Donner invited him to Bali. He needed time off, some self-reflection, and a fresh perspective in life.

He thought of the secret game he was now a part of—"The Globalist." He has been a top achiever in the business arena but had nothing to show in the sociocivic landscape. Probably easy for John Donner to figure it out, resulting in the invitation. Perhaps it was high time to give back. It was time for him to make another mark in the world and to find out more about its true meaning.

But what project should he pursue? In order to really make a difference, he felt he should pick a project that is radical and unusual—something nobody ever thought of before. His business philosophy was to always pursue something intrinsically simple and easy to implement. Complexity is an ingredient for disaster. He never needed to develop laborious business plans or even conduct research for any of his ventures. Simple mathematical calculations would instantly tell him whether a business model would work or not. Some claim to possess a gut feel for business—he'd called it common sense. He always wondered why other people failed to see opportunities and threats in their simplest forms.

But what social project? Food, he thought, was best. The basic human needs are food, clothing, and shelter, in that order. If the foremost need was not met, there can be no life.

Lack of food threatens health and life. He wondered how many millions were starving out there.

Steve Blake thought of the vast amount of food that goes to waste in the buffet tables in his hotels, casinos, and cruise lines. All that food is thrown away at the end of the day. His companies must have been throwing away millions of dollars worth of food annually.

All the thrown-out food in the world might actually add up to billions of dollars, if you consider all restaurants and hotels worldwide.

He remembered his own hunger-filled days as a young boy. Surely, he would have loved to eat the excess food in the buffet tables, even if it was slightly stale. Man, he thought, most of the food thrown away in his companies was not even close to stale. Hotels and restaurants have to throw them out for fear that they might get sued or their reputation besmirched if someone gets an upset stomach. Darn it, he thought, who on Earth would care about an upset stomach when one is starving to death?

His mind envisioned the starving children in Africa. Would these children turn down a slightly stale McDonald's burger, a donut from Dunkin' Donuts, or a steak from one of his hotels? What about those in prison cells in poor countries? Or those patients in dilapidated government hospitals? Or those in war-torn areas?

It was a question of logistics and distribution, he thought. Getting the food to the right people, from where it is abundant to where it is scarce. It was a question of getting rid of the name-brand mentality and the fear of ruining a company's reputation.

"What if we put brands aside?" he thought. "What if the food will be labeled, say 'xF,' boxed up decently, marked, stored well, and then distributed to starving or deprived people across international communities?"

Steve Blake's heart pumped faster. He marveled and laughed at the thought. I've just created another global brand—"xF Foods." Motto: "Slightly stale Big Mac with a conscience."

He remembered reading somewhere that breakfast was the most important meal of the day. He also read in an article that millions of children worldwide had difficulty in school because they went to school hungry. True, how can one think well when one is hungry?

Perhaps he can put the two together. He can form the "Breakfast for the World" foundation to feed the millions of starving children and deprived individuals worldwide with "xF Food." Food that is put aside by hotels and restaurants at midnight, when stored and kept properly, would still be good by 7:00 a.m. the following day—in time for breakfast.

Now he was ecstatic. When was the last time he felt like this? When he produced his first entertainment show? His first hotel? The entrepreneur inside him was screaming inside. It was a very simple concept, yet how come no one ever thought about it? How come no one is doing it?

There were issues to consider. First, an alliance with potential food contributors was necessary. Australia and New Zealand would not be a problem. Since he was a former national head of the Hotel and Restaurant Association, getting others to participate would not be a problem. The second issue involved logistics—getting the food wrapped, stored, and delivered to the right people in time for breakfast. He thought about soliciting support from FedEx, United Parcel Service, and airlines. Surely, up to 50 pounds of donated food would not be a problem for these carriers. Thirdly, potential intermediaries such as churches, volunteer groups, governments, schools, and even sociocivic organizations would only be too happy to help in the distribution. These entities could also help identify the most deprived sectors of the society.

He needed to build and organize a global network—an interconnected web of like-minded organizations sharing a common vision. A tough project, but not impossible.

Yes, the Breakfast for the World Foundation. Perhaps he could even get his ex-wives and his grown-up children involved in the project. Unlike him, they have all had some involvement in sociocivic projects. In addition, they were all already masters in the art of spending his money.

He picked up his mobile phone and made the first call.

Dr. Pete Omalu: Democratization of Medicine

"Announcing the arrival of South African Airways Flight No. 287, direct flight from Hong Kong," boomed a friendly female voice from the airport intercom.

Dr. Pete Omalu stepped off the aircraft and slowly walked across the tarmac. He felt rather weary. It had been a long flight, but one that had allowed him a lot of time to think and plan out his international agenda.

He waived at his deputy, Dr. Carl Saunders. As usual, Carl had his bags taken care of and his limousine ready. He walked toward Carl and shook his hand.

"How are you, Carl?"

"Great, Pete. How was your flight and vacation?"

"Couldn't be better. Spent a lot of time thinking."

"Not about all the work at home, I hope." Carl looked concerned. He had encouraged Pete to take on the invitation of John Donner primarily because he felt the doctor was working too hard. Their research project had been proceeding at full steam, and they had been putting in 16-hour days for the past 2 months. He had taken his brief vacation in London a month earlier and felt Pete deserved a big vacation himself.

"No, not so much about work," Pete replied. "Actually, more about new directions."

"Sounds interesting. The limousine is ready. I'll ride with you, and we can talk, if you wish."

"Excellent. Let's go." They walked toward the limousine at the curbside.

"So, how's Bali? I heard the beaches there are great," Carl continued.

"Yes, great beaches and great food. I even took time out for a traditional Asian massage," Pete said teasingly.

"Stop already. I'm turning green with envy."

Pete smiled briefly. "Speaking of green, how's the herbal research going?"

"We're progressing well and ahead of schedule. The lab team discovered a few more enzymes that could speed up the assimilation of the herbal product in the bloodstream. We're right on track. As expected, the prolonged intake of the herb has continued to minimize the exhibited symptoms of our AIDS patients. We've continued the test on a new batch of patients since you left; about half of them are now up and about. No side effects observed."

"I expected that. What about the supply side?"

"Looks like the herb is more abundant than we thought. It's widely available all over Africa. Our team's latest estimate is that 1,275 metric tons of the herb may be available to us in a year. It would be more than enough to serve the regional requirement. We can even export some."

"Good. I spoke with the ministers of the Department of Agriculture in Indonesia, Malaysia, the Philippines, and Papua New Guinea. It looks like they have similar strains of the herb there."

"Gosh, Pete, that's excellent news!"

"It is. Imagine a world where we have can have treatment pills for AIDS at less than 10 U.S. cents, and one without side effects."

Both were suddenly quiet. Both were simultaneously thinking through different ramifications of their project. Carl was thinking about the supply side. Pete was thinking about the global distribution. They have worked on the project for over 3 years now; it has become part of their daily lives.

Pete broke the silence. "It's time we took our herb globally, Carl."

"I really doubt that's going to work. We talked about that before. There are tough medical compliance laws in developed countries. We could face lawsuits."

"I know that. What we're going to do is set up distribution centers in countries that are open to them and that offer strong government support. We'll tap two or three in each region, and patients can buy the herbal pills from these regional centers. This way, the pills become more accessible and patients don't have to travel to Africa to get them."

"That might work, but which governments would want to be a part of it?"

"There would be several, I would imagine. AIDS has been a headache in several locations, and worse, it drastically affects the poorer segments. The ones that can least afford the growingly expensive medication. We'll need to find the right alliances in our chosen regional locations."

"The plan would cost a lot of money, Pete."

"Oh c'mon, Carl. We have money—and more funding is underway." Pete's mind raced—he found the right project for "The Globalist" competition. He would set up regional centers for the cure of AIDS. Interestingly, the activity is well aligned with his current line of work and builds on its existing core competence. Furthermore, he has a huge base of industry networks and contacts to build on. This could be a smooth and easy ride. He thought of the millions of patients that would be helped. "Excellent," he thought. "I'll be hitting two birds with one stone. I'm expanding my company, while gaining a good shot at the $35 million pot money." He wondered if his competitors could come up with projects that could beat his international social platform. He glanced briefly at Carl and deliberated for a minute on whether he should let his trusted aide know about the game he got himself into. What would Carl think? He decided it was best to keep the details of the game to himself, as agreed upon in Bali.

Elena Chavez: Fashionable Cause

"Yes, mama, I'm fine," Elena spoke loudly through her mobile phone. She was by her house pool in a luxurious villa in Brazil. The sun blazed warmly, scattering vibrant colors across the inviting swimming pool. It's been 1 week since the Bali meeting.

The competition has caused her stress over the past few days. She couldn't come up with any appropriate idea for the project. She has never been involved, nor has shown interest, in social causes. Rather than proceeding to her New York office, she felt a trip to her family's house in Brazil might help clear her thoughts and allow her to focus better.

The check she issued for $5 million in Bali was not totally funded. She had to borrow money from her father to make sure that it clears when deposited in a bank. She felt pressured by "The Globalist" challenge.

Where on Earth did John Donner get the idea that she had that kind of money? Yes, she owns properties and a fashion empire, but she is hardly liquid. Most of her resources were tied to long-term investments. She also had a gnawing debt problem. Fortunately, her father bailed her out twice in the past 6 months. She needed to win the competition, if only to improve her cash position.

The past few days had been hectic. She had to catch up with work and make sure that bills were paid. She wished she didn't have this competition to deal with. Again, fortunately, her mother has been an able and supportive business partner.

"Mama, I can't go to New York right now," she continued in an irritated manner. "You'll have to deal with it yourself, please—*por favor?*" She rolled her eyes upward.

A lady servant brought in a tray of pastries, fruits, and orange juice.

Elena shifted her sitting position and propped her legs on top of the adjacent chair. She nodded at her servant and mumbled a voiceless "*gracias*" with a smile. The servant responded with a smile and walked away quietly.

"Mom, I may need to travel extensively in the next few months. I've committed myself . . . No, not to a man. It's a special project. I'll let you know once I firm up the details. Meanwhile, it might be a good idea to start looking for a competent manager to support our business expansion in North America." She sat quietly, listening intently for a few minutes, and then added, "Okay, I'll talk to you later mama. *Até logo.*"

She turned off the phone and sipped on her juice. Her thoughts shifted to Bali and "The Globalist" competition. With a table pen, she scribbled the words "greatest global impact" on a paper napkin. She drummed her fingers and looked around her father's vast estate. The poolside was a replica of an island paradise.

Then, a thought struck her. Hundreds, perhaps thousands of beach communities need help. Natural beaches are being eroded by careless commercial expansion and pollution, marine life destroyed by dynamite fishing. Some of the ethnic cultures and value systems are adulterated by media exposure. If financial resources are available, nature may be conserved in these communities and indigenous cultural systems can be nurtured and further cultivated.

She got it. She will create a new fashion line to be called "Islander Fashions." This line will showcase beach crafts, clothing, and fashion accessories from beach communities around the world. Ten, perhaps 20, percent of the item's price shall go into an "Islander Nature Conservation Fund." The fund shall address issues and concerns plaguing beach communities worldwide. Customers automatically belong to an "Islander's Club," where they can get special discounts in resorts in exotic beach communities. These resorts can be recruited as sponsors and can even carry the fashion line in their gift shops. Airlines, tourism boards, and cruise lines can join as sponsors. In effect, she builds a unique clothing line, enhances customer loyalty through a club, gathers support from private and government entities, while helping millions around the world.

All stakeholders have something to gain as venture participants: customers get a quality product while supporting a cause, corporate sponsors build a customer base and improve their image, governments and tourism boards get to promote a beach destination and help local communities, hotels and resorts boost profits from the product, the company earns money, and beach communities are helped.

"This seems great," she thought, "and enjoyable, too." Even if she doesn't get "The Globalist" prize, the venture could have the potential to earn over $35 million in a span of a few years. This could be her best and biggest venture yet.

She speed dials on her mobile phone. "Hi, papa," she says sweetly. "We need to talk."

Sabrina Lopez: Keeping Families Together

Sabrina's heart bled at the Ninoy Aquino International Airport in Manila, Philippines. As she waited for her limousine at the airport's arrival area, she stood witness to thousands of family members eagerly anticipating the arrival of loved ones. Sons, daughters, spouses, siblings, mothers, and fathers—stretching their bodies eagerly, expecting to see a loved one who has been away for years, working in a foreign country

She focused her attention on a nice-looking family: a young wife standing alongside three children, about ages 10, 7, and 5. An elderly couple stood behind her, presumably the husband's parents. Soon, a thin, middle-aged man stepped onto the curb. The family jumps in unison and screams excitedly. "Daddy, Carlo, *anak* . . ." The mother and wife break into tears of joy. The middle-aged man runs toward the steel trellis, hugs his wife and kids, and cries.

Sabrina stared away, not to avoid embarrassment but to prevent herself from crying. Tears welled in her eyes. She wondered how long this man Carlo may have been away from his family. And how long before the family would cry again, with tears of sorrow, when Carlo has to depart again.

She looked through the entire length of the arrival gate. There were thousands like Carlo. She remembered reading an article the previous month that mentioned there are over 7 million overseas foreign workers in the Philippines—Filipinos who take on contractual work in other countries in order to provide for their families back home. She wondered what this separation does to families; she anguished at the thought of the pain and sacrifice the family had to go through together in order to be able to eat and earn a decent living.

She felt for Carlo and the young family. She remembered the pain she experienced as a young child when her father passed away. The trauma of the loss has stayed with her in her entire life. Despite her attractive looks and sterling career success as an Asian venture capitalist, she never considered settling down, All because of the fear of losing a loved one once again.

Sabrina stole a glimpse of Carlo's weeping 5-year-old daughter, who was now embracing and clinging to her father's legs. She could have been that child in another place and time.

Her anguish was interrupted. "Ms. Lopez? Ma'am, your limousine is ready. Can I help you with your bags?"

"Yes, thank you," Sabrina managed to mumble.

"Are you okay, ma'am?"

"Yes. Get me to Oakwood Towers as soon as possible."

"Yes, ma'am. Right away."

Sabrina sat quietly throughout the trip. She thought through the mechanics of her new endeavor. Over the next few months, she will create the Overseas Foreign Worker Venture Fund, which will offer capital for business ideas of overseas workers planning to return home to rejoin their families. Her target will be contract workers in the Philippines and neighboring Southeast Asia. Substantial profit has to be generated in order to keep the project sustainable. In this manner, more will continue to benefit in the future. Training programs, as well as monitoring and support systems, have to be in place to improve the likelihood of success of the recipients of capital. She would need to work through political, cultural, and business barriers that may exist in a country like the Philippines. There are obstacles, but there are also opportunities that can lead to success. Adjustments have to be made to deal with the challenges existing in the country. After Southeast Asia, she will spin off the fund globally, making a positive impact on even more lives.

James Edwards: Country Business

It was his fourth glass of Scotch, and James Edwards was in a jolly mood.

"Of course not!" he shouted aloud. "There is absolutely no bloody way this country would ever change."

The man seated across the pub table, Charles Spalding, snorted, "Get out of here. Reforms need to be made to adjust to a changing global environment. Not a single country is spared by globalization!"

"Tell me then—what political changes have you seen across Europe? How has it improved, pray tell?" Customers in the upscale London bar started giving them stolen glances—the duo had been at it for over an hour now.

"Plenty—trade liberalization, technologies that improve cross-border communication, labor dynamics, quality of products and services—I could go on the whole night . . ."

"Well," James cleared his throat and stopped to stub his cigarette. "How about the social system? The standard of living of the population? Health care? The drug problem? I could go on the whole night as well."

"Fine!" Charles interjected loudly. "If you really think you know best, why don't you run this country?" Equally inebriated customers stared at them in disgust.

"You know what?" James cut in. "You know what . . . ? You may have just given me an idea. I'm going to buy my own country."

"I think you've had too much to drink, James."

"I'm serious. Hypothetically . . . hypothetically . . . if you offer to buy a small island country somewhere in the Pacific that is deep in depth . . . I mean, debt . . . wouldn't the leader consider selling it? You can then set your own rules, take it global, and commercialize it. Turn it into the smoothest, global-ready city. Market it, sell country bonds at Wall Street, hype it up."

"You're insane."

"You can make it entirely free-trade friendly, no tariffs, no barriers. Everything investors want. Like Hong Kong, without the traffic and congestion, no visas and passports required, and far cheaper real estate rentals."

"Don't forget to take some Alka-Seltzer tomorrow morning when you get up."

"State-of-the-art technologies, alongside white sandy beaches. Legalized gambling, tax holidays—the global investor's paradise. You can even change its name to increase its marketability."

"Okay, assuming it's technically possible, what leader, in his sane mind, would give up his country and people?"

"Ahhh . . . that's easy. A country that is deep in debt, facing a political crisis, and totally out of its league in the global arena. Possibly a small population that is needy. I'll have to sell the concept to the leader—sell the sizzle. The leader can stay as a titular head, I don't really care. I can transform the place; I own it after all—lock, stock, and barrel. Then sell it at Wall Street. I can see it now—Las Vegas meets Silicon Valley meets Hong Kong in a Pacific Island. Yipee!!!!"

James was ecstatic. Charles gave him a crazy look.

"Charles, I can change world dynamics by taking on this country! Impact the lives of millions, create new millionaires! You don't believe I could do this, do you?"

"Definitely not—I am starting to have doubts about your mental health, James. I've always known you to be a risk taker and some sort of a maverick. You may have to see a psychiatrist sometime soon. This is plain dumb and preposterous—way beyond just drunk."

"Fine, then," James countered. "Let's make a bet. I bet a million pounds that I can buy a country somewhere in the world and show you a deed of sale within 3 months."

"You're on. Let's make it 5 million pounds," Charles added.

"It's a deal." James smiled; for a moment he felt sorry for his best friend—he knew he could get himself a country. But then again, Charles is a very rich man—5 million pounds is a drop in the bucket. He could also use the money as his play capital to really drum up the global island paradise. He'll have to start looking for a country to buy, fast. Could his competitors beat owning and running a country and providing it with global freedom? He doubted it. The opportunities are endless.

Road to Global Transformation

It was a cold evening in New York. Exactly 8 months to the day since the competitors met in Bali, John Donner was seated at his desk in his home library.

In the past few months, he had paid for the services of a prestigious private investigator to check and document the activities of all competitors. The investigator traveled all over the world and prepared a film documentary and written report on the group's activities. He had read the written report earlier in the day and was about to view the film. The investigator had told him that the documentary contained brief media interviews that indicated what the six other individuals have been doing.

John loaded the film in the DVD player, picked up the remote control, and sat on of the office couch. He pressed "play."

Jack Wang Interview

Media Correspondent: *Mr. Wang, how would you explain the phenomenal success of the Asian Charity and Insurance Fund, or ACIF?*

Jack Wang: It is high time that the business community seeks the convergence of profitability and social sensitivity. I did this project with the sheer intention of looking into the needs of the underprivileged. I did not anticipate the tremendous support by the media, the governments, and private corporations in many parts of the world. This venture fund operates under a unique model and created its own niche. I believe this contributed largely to its success.

Media Correspondent: *There has been so much speculation on the number of members worldwide that have availed of the insurance service of ACIF; can you provide us with an accurate figure?*

Jack Wang: I regret the exact number is confidential, but let me tell you that we now have over 300,000 members worldwide.

Media Correspondent: *Can you provide us with a sense of the future corporate direction of ACIF?*

Jack Wang: The company is expanding globally. We are looking to tap into even the most remote regions in the world and are currently building strategic alliances . . .

John Donner smiled; he missed his friend. He was glad to see Jack healthy and apparently happy. He pressed number two on the remote control.

Steve Blake

TV Host: *We're here tonight with a special guest—real estate and entertainment czar and now dedicated philanthropist—Mr. Steve Blake. How are you, Steve?*

Steve Blake: I'm fine, Jerry, thank you.

TV Host: *I meant to ask you, with your intense international efforts in the Breakfast for the World Foundation, are you slowing down on the business expansion of your hotel chain and media empire?*

Steve Blake: Not really, Jerry. I have competent top-level managers implementing our corporate expansion plans throughout the world. At this stage in my life, I am merely devoting attention to a social cause that can impact the global community.

TV Host: *Why the sudden change of focus? Has there been a life-changing event that stirred this social interest?*

Steve Blake: Not really, I guess it was just a matter of time. It could have happened to me earlier, or even later, in my life. But this desire for social change has happened to me now, and I feel the timing couldn't have been better.

TV Host: *Any plans for a career in politics?*

Steve Blake: [laughs] Not really, I'm pretty happy with the way things are, and I don't need further complications.

John Donner pressed pause and looked at Steve's smiling face on the television. He looked younger and invigorated. He remembered reading about the Breakfast for the World Foundation in a business magazine the previous week. Steve received accolades from government and religious leaders worldwide. Even without winning "The Globalist" secret competition, he may well become a prime candidate for the Nobel Peace Prize. He was amazed at the speed by which the competitors could make things happen. Transferring successful business principles to a social cause can lead to a potent combination. He pressed the number three on the remote control.

On Dr. Steve Omalu

TV Host: *What are your thoughts on the widespread availability of the Herbalove products?*

Guest 1: As an executive in the pharmaceutical industry, I believe the product needs to be further tested for potential side effects. To be a global drug, conformity to standards and legal implications need to be thoroughly considered. We don't need another quack doctor or fake medicine on the market.

Guest 2: Have you been reading medical journals at all? The founder of Herbalove, Dr. Omalu, is a well-respected physician and researcher. Herbalove has helped thousands in the deprived sectors of our society.

Guest 1: I'm not arguing about Dr. Omalu's competence or intent; what I'm saying is that like all drugs in the market, there are procedures that have to be followed.

Guest 2: AIDS and cancer can't wait. Besides, who decides on the standards? The U.S. FDA? What gives the U.S. government the right to decide on applicable standards for the entire international community? Should the U.S. government decide on the prices as well? And the brand names?

Host: *Excuse me for interrupting, how many do you think have used or benefited from Herbalove?*

Guest 2: My guess is it should be over a million now.

John Donner pressed the stop button on the remote. He was pensive. He read the investigator's written report earlier and was bothered by the fact that Dr. Omalu is facing several lawsuits as a result of the introduction of Herbalove. He wondered whether the global distribution of the medicine was a result of Dr. Omalu's original corporate strategy or a response to "The Globalist" game. The large pharmaceutical companies are on his back and are deeply concerned that Dr. Omalu's success might be a negative industry precedent. The issue was highly volatile and there were so many parties involved. He worried whether someone was keeping track of Dr. Omalu's every move. What if someone eventually tracks his trip to Bali and associates it with the activities of the others? "The Globalist" secret competition may be compromised and could face the risk of exposure. He cringed at the thought of the drastic implications to himself and all the other competitors. He pressed number four.

Elena Chavez

The video clip showed excerpts of a glamorous Islander Fashion advertisement, a fashion show where the Islander product lines were featured, an MTV video clip, and an airline and tourism joint endorsement of Islander Fashion.

John Donner pressed "fast-forward" until Elena's face appeared. It was an interview on a nature channel.

> **Elena Chavez:** Yes, a portion of the Islander Fashion's proceeds do, in fact, go to beach communities. Our vision is to marry our business with social responsibility.
>
> **TV Host:** *How have the beach communities been helped?*
>
> **Elena Chavez:** We use a portion of our earnings to protect and conserve the beach environment, cultivate culture, help create jobs, and promote and enhance the image of exotic beach destinations.
>
> **TV Host:** *If you'll look to the side of the screen, you'll see the video footage of some of the beach communities you have helped. Aside from helping the locals and the obvious clean up, what may have been your contribution to the marine life in these communities?*
>
> **Elena Chavez:** I failed to mention that our corporate mascot is a whale. [laughs]. Marine life conservation runs parallel to our mission. As we protect coral reefs and clean up the beaches, we are in fact also contributing to the long-term sustainability of the islands. While we've helped thousands of people, we've helped millions of marine life.

On Sabrina Lopez

News Reporter: In other business news, venture capitalist
Sabrina Lopez met with the president and key government
labor officials to discuss the broadening of the scope of implementation of the Overseas Foreign Worker Venture Fund
Since the fund was launched last year, over 100,000 foreign
workers opted to avail of the fund. The fund has been attributed to the stimulation of entrepreneurial activity in smaller
cities across the country. Due to the fund's success, discussions
are underway to also allow Philippine migrants who migrated
to other countries years ago to avail of the fund and return to
the country to start a business.

John Donner smiled. It looks like Sabrina found her calling. He read
in the written report that Sabrina is presently engaged to a local gentle-
man. Interestingly, the young fellow, named Gabriel Santos, is a former
foreign worker whose venture Sabrina funded. Gabriel has successfully
built a multimillion-dollar enterprise in a span of a few months, through
Sabrina's help and guidance.

On James Edwards

The television screen showed excerpts of a reality television show entitled
Building a Country.

Host: Maverick entrepreneur and consultant James Edwards
dreamt of an island paradise: an investor's haven and entertainment mecca situated alongside white sandy beaches.
While others merely dream, he turned the dream into reality: the Isle of Mars. Follow James Edwards as he pursues
his dream in creating the ultimate country. Last week, we
witnessed the completion of the high-tech wonders and the
opening of the second phase of the theme park and casino. In
today's episode, we shall track the visit of key Wall Street players and rating executives and seek their views on the suitability
of the country as an investment haven.

John Donner laughed. He knew about James Edwards's exploits—it was all over the news. He didn't know about the reality show. This world can be strange and funny.

He thought of his own project and tried to measure how he stood against the rest. His newly formed company, Gulf Peace Technologies, has been a success. He has gained ground throughout the Middle East. It was not easy since he had to deal with incidents involving the kidnapping of one his employees, theft, and the burning of one facility. Nevertheless, they were relatively minor cases. He continued to face these threats on a daily basis. Yet he knew he has gained serious ground and uplifted the lives of thousands. He knew he contributed to a favorable image of America and was extremely thankful for the support of the government and private sector.

With regard to "The Globalist" competition, he knew all of them were winners. Each project changed the world somehow and changed the lives of all protagonists to some extent. He was pleased with each one's progress.

He rose and sat on his desk. He drew a table to gauge where each of them stood and to try to determine who was on track to win the game.

He assessed the competitors once more. Steve Blake is likely in the lead because of a technicality. If he provided one breakfast to a person, he spared the person from hunger, therefore making an impact on a life, although the impact is very short term. Dr. Omalu's impact is widespread and literally saves lives. He should rank about the same as Jack Wang and Sabrina Lopez. However, both of them have a way of documenting their contribution. It is harder for Dr. Omalu to do so. Elena is definitely behind, though her project was a huge commercial success and impacted

Name	Project	Estimated impact
Jack Wang	Asian Charity and Insurance Fund	2,000,000 lives
Steve Blake	Breakfast for the World Foundation	5,000,000 lives
Dr. Pete Omalu	Herbalove	3,000,000 lives
Elena Chavez	Islander Fashion	1,000,000 lives
Sabrina Lopez	Overseas Foreign Worker Venture Fund	2,000,000 lives
James Edwards	Isle of Mars	undetermined
John Donner	Gulf Peace Technologies	2,000,000 lives

hundreds and thousands of lives, it will be tough to concretely measure. However, her impact on marine life and the environment is profound and has far-reaching implications. It is impossible to determine the impact of James Edwards's project. It would be a mistake to court him out, as the guy is full of surprises.

The final meeting in Bali is exactly 4 months away—things can still change for everybody. He marveled at the thought of how many lives were touched in 8 months as a result of the competition. He was thrilled at the thought of how several millions more will be helped in the coming months.

The Eve of Truth

They were once again gathered around the campfire in Bali. All were somewhat quiet, as if in deep thought. This was, after all, a moment of truth: the culmination of a yearlong challenge.

All of them had given their best; all had put in a significant amount of personal resources. Some had put their reputations at stake; others, their sanity. All faced serious obstacles head-on; all changed their attitudes and perspectives in life.

John Donner spoke, "Well ladies, gentlemen, this is it—the end of the road. It was a hell of a ride, wasn't it?"

"Oh, you bet it was!" James Edwards added gleefully. "Glad we did it."

The rest smiled.

John Donner continued, "Okay, then, let us begin. Each of us will be given an opportunity to speak for about 10 minutes to articulate why he or she deserves to be 'The Globalist.' In the interest of time, there will be no interruptions. After everyone has spoken, we shall then secretly vote by writing the name of our selected globalist on a piece of paper. No one is to vote for oneself. As agreed, the winner is adjudged "The Globalist." The person gets the pot money of $35 million, and everyone's support for future recognition. As you may have realized by now, the honor of being appointed 'The Globalist' tonight is not just about wealth and fame; it's about being the person who has done the greatest good to our global community. It's about being the person who has really changed the world the most and was voted upon by equally deserving peers. Let's proceed clockwise; Jack, let's start with you."

Jack smiled nervously and then stood up. "Good evening, everyone. My name is Jack Wang, and I am a globalist. The initiative I launched last year, called the Asian Charity and Insurance Fund, provided accident insurance to workers who couldn't afford it. These workers were located in poor communities across Asia, and their companies are not mandated to, or refuse to, provide this type of insurance. I wanted to help these workers by providing them and their families with a financial safety net in the event of an accident. The venture has been profitable, but more importantly, it has protected 7,255 accident victims in barely a year of operation. There have been 788,422 workers recruited into the program to date. I have all their names in a folder in my briefcase. Assuming each worker had a family of four, the project made an impact on the lives of at least 3,153,688. Thank you, and your vote is appreciated."

Steve Blake stood up. "Hello, everyone. I'm Steve Blake from Australia. I, too, am a globalist—perhaps more of one than the preceding competitor, Jack Wang. Last year, I launched the Breakfast for the World Foundation. The objective of the program was to feed the impoverished in urban locations and depressed areas around the world. The concept was simple—I gathered all the food that was about to be thrown away in many parts of the world, packaged it as "xF," and sent it off to needy locations in the fastest way possible. It was all about using the currently efficient global supply and distribution system, matching them with the right technology and organizational support, and getting the machinery rolling. The program exploded as a result of strong support and media hype worldwide. Strong corporate support from airlines, hotels, casinos, restaurants, foundations, and governments has made the project sustainable. As of yesterday, the program fed roughly 10,250,000 people. I do not have the exact names of all beneficiaries, but I do have networks that account and monitor the exact number of goods that were distributed. If we are looking specifically at numbers, I believe I won this competition. I seek your vote; thank you."

Dr. Pete Omalu stood up. "Good evening. With utmost humility, I call myself a globalist. This competition has changed me, as well as my perspective in life, perhaps in the same way as with most of you. Like Steve, I created a global product. My product consisted of a range of herbal medications and pills under the name brand of Herbalove. Using my company's technology and capital resources, I facilitated the distribution of the Herbalove pills to regional centers in all continents. In turn, the regional centers became trans-shipment points to the poorer communities worldwide. The strategic location and efficient distribution facilitated global accessibility of the product and made the medicines very affordable for AIDS and cancer patients. My company sold 110 million capsules of Herbalove last year. I cannot specifically document the number of lives that have been saved, but I can claim a customer base of close to 3 million worldwide. If we count the families of patients as secondary beneficiaries of this global initiative, then perhaps over 10 million lives haves been touched by Herbalove. I do not claim to be a true altruist or even a philanthropist; I am a scientist and a health facilitator with an entrepreneurial streak. As a result of the product, the company has been very profitable. More importantly, the product I have created literally saved lives and made a huge difference in the global society. Having said that, I am counting on your vote."

It was Elena Chaves's turn to speak. "Hi, I'm Elena. This time last year, making a social impact may have been the last thing on mind. I have lived a privileged life and had a fairly successful business career; little else mattered. This competition truly changed my life and business perspective. I learned that one can, in fact, balance business success and social responsibility. The company I created, Islander Fashion, offers concrete evidence. I wanted to create a fashion empire that simultaneously supported the needs of struggling beach communities in exotic locations around the world. I gave a portion of my corporate profits to the cause, created a support club, and developed strategic alliances with numerous government and private enterprises. The company earned over $50 million last year, and I gave $10 million to beach communities. I received $20 million more in corporate sponsorships and support and used most of the money to educate people on the need to protect marine life. The company helped over a million people; more importantly, it saved, and continues to save, perhaps hundreds of millions of marine creatures. The future impact cannot be measured, but it is huge. I want you all to know that I carried out this venture with little money but lots of conviction. I am not as rich as all of you, and I worked so hard to make this happen. Ultimately, it was no longer about the competition, but rather what I really believed in. You don't have to vote for me. Others truly deserve the honor more. I am happy and content with the path I have taken the past year, and know deep in my heart—that in my own very small way—I, too, am a globalist."

Sabrina Lopez stood up and gave Elena a hug. "Thank you, Elena. I have a story to share. Once there was a young girl who adored her father. The man meant the world to her. She prayed for him very night, painted pictures of him, wrote poems for him, got 'A' grades in school for him. In turn, the father brought home candies for the little girl every time he came home from work. It was routine—a candy everyday at 6:00 p.m. One day, the girl waited until it was 7:00 p.m., and the father was not home; then it was 8:00 p.m. 'Where was the candy?' she wondered. That night, she went to sleep crying. Where was her father? Why wasn't he around? Why didn't she get her candy that night? She learned the next day that her father had died in an accident. After work, he was run over by a truck as he crossed the street to the neighborhood store to buy candy. That girl's life has never been, and will never be, the same again . . . I was that little girl, and last year I came across a project that allowed me to reunite fathers, mothers, sisters, brothers, and children with their families. In the Philippines, millions of family members leave their loved ones to find work in other countries. They do this not because they want to, but out of desperation to find jobs and because of the lack of capital available to start a business. As a consequence, some of these people die under the employ of unscrupulous employers; many end up divorced. I set up the Overseas Foreign Worker Venture Fund in the Philippines so that these overseas workers will have the option to stay home with their families and run a business. In barely a year, the fund has supplied the capital requirements of 420,000 overseas workers in the country and in the neighboring Southeast Asian locations. Close to 2 million family members were positively affected, not to mention the impact of job creation on the 420,000 businesses created in the region, and the subsequent impact on their families. Better yet, since the Philippine labor force stays in the country, the jobs that they would have taken in international locations may have stayed with the local citizens, limiting job displacement. The venture has global implications. My plan is to replicate the model globally. In this context, I was, am, and will always be a globalist."

James Edwards stood up and pat Sabrina lightly on the back. "Now, how can anyone beat that? Hmmm . . . But I can, and I have. Nice effort chaps; regretfully, though, there can only be one globalist, and you're looking at him. As you all know, I am now a prime minister and rightful owner of a country—the Isle of Mars. This competition led me into buying a country that all can enjoy. Getting the country was the easy part; building it was a horrendous experience. The country has a small population, actually, hmmm . . . about 5,000; no, 4,994, to be exact. I believe six died last week in a boat accident. Nevertheless, the county . . . I mean country . . . had good infrastructure—the rocks were rather solid (strong ground support), surrounded by ocean (shipping potential), several large trees (construction supply) . . . I convinced the president to sell it to me for half a million pounds. Everything on it—including the presidential palace, more of a hut, really, and the presidential yacht disguised as a raft. Well, we then had a county . . . I mean a country referendum where I was appointed prime minister and was empowered to change and create all laws. This is where my brilliance kicked in. I turned the island paradise into an investor's haven. It had everything a global investor wanted in a country and more. I sold the country's bonds at Wall Street and launched a global advertising and marketing campaign. I brought in casino operators, Silicon Valley executives, entertainment giants, diplomats—soon the place was awash with big-time investors. Imagine a country that offered tax holidays, absolute free trade, no trade barriers, legalized gambling and drugs, latest technologies, beachfront estates—the works. I now own and control the ultimate global city— the new frontier of globalization. In barely a year, the Isle of Mars, earned about 500 million pounds in advance payments, taxes, real estate deals, royalties, and whatever we can earn from. As prime minister, I took out 100 million pounds and distributed it to 100 countries—1 million pounds each for governments to undertake sociocivic projects that are the most important to them. I gave the last one just yesterday—all given in the spirit of goodwill from the Isle of Mars. I figured governments would know better what their country really needs, perhaps more than I ever will. Let's see, I gave documented donations to the United States, China, India, the United Kingdom—wouldn't that be over a billion people now benefiting from my kind contribution? Ladies and gentlemen, I rest my case—I am 'The Globalist.'"

Everyone around the campfire was dumbfounded.

John Donner rose and stretched his legs. "Who would think that a group of relatively young people, gathered around a campfire a year ago, can impact the lives of billions around the world? Guess it's my turn. My project is not as elaborate and brilliant as John's. In fact, it is quite simple. I set up a company called Gulf Peace Technologies. My objective was to foster peace in the Middle East by providing people with technology and educating them. I also wanted to get them tied into a strand of the web of globalization. This way, many will be aware and appreciate the merits of globalization and will learn to profit from it. I wanted to help people in these countries eventually become better educated and financially independent, as a means of curbing global terrorism. Terrorism spans the globe and affects all of us—every single person in every single country. So far, I've documented 750,000 specific beneficiaries in the venture; 2,200 were former members of terrorist cells. These individuals have been trained in computer technologies, and my organization has helped them find gainful employment. The venture is relatively new but has spread fast. I am unsure how many lives will be ultimately saved, but I am confident of its favorable overall global impact. It has helped curb terrorism and cultivated peace in many countries. Like all of you, my life has also changed as a result of this clandestine competition. I believe all of you, all of us, are winners and are globalists. The contribution we've made to the world is astounding. I have acted as initiator and moderator of this group; in some way, I fear this might influence your vote. I am therefore withdrawing my name from the competition. As we select 'The Globalist,' please do not vote for me. It might be best that I do not vote as well. Consider my $5 million as a personal donation to the pot money. I shall be more than happy to lend support and live up to my commitment to whoever is selected as 'The Globalist.' Is this acceptable?"

Everyone nodded quietly.

"Well then, shall we start?"

John Donner passed around pieces of paper and six pens.

"Please write the name of your selected globalist on the piece of paper. After you've written the name, please pass the slip of paper back to me. I will then read the votes to the group. The person getting the most votes wins. We will do a second vote in the event of a tie. The group's decision is final. Let's have 15 minutes to think; no discussions please. Good luck to all."

Everyone around the campfire sat quietly and still.

"May I have your votes now, please?"

John Donner gathered the six slips of paper and shuffled them.

He picked out one and read, "James Edwards—one vote."

He picked out another. "Pete Omalu—one vote."

"Steve Blake—one vote."

"Jack Wang—one vote."

"Sabrina Lopez—one vote."

John paused. "I'm pretty sure none of you voted for oneself. I've been watching each of you. This leaves one more vote, and whoever gets two votes automatically wins."

Everyone sat tensely and braced themselves for the announcement. The prospect of losing $5 million or gaining $35 million of the pot money is enough to stir excitement in anyone. Won money can speed up their new ventures; a loss of $5 million can slow them down.

John picked out the last vote, read, and smiled. "Elena Chavez—one vote."

Everyone was astonished. It was a six-way tie.

James Edwards exclaimed, "Wait a minute, that can't be right. It's as if we all won!"

John Donner smiled, "Exactly. Congratulations globalists. It's a strange and amusing world, isn't it?"

He handed back the $5 million dollar check to each of them and pocketed his own.

Notes

Chapter 1

1. Greenberg and Baron (1997).
2. Bartlett and Ghoshal (1998).
3. Friedman (2005).
4. Friedman (2000).
5. Guillen and Garcia-Canal (2009).
6. Botman (2004).
7. Bornstein (2004).
8. Fowler (2000).
9. Social Enterprise Alliance (2009).
10. R. Harding (personal communication, June 19, 2009).
11. Waddock and Post (1991).
12. Ashoka Foundation (2004).
13. Mort, Weerawardena, and Carnegie (2003).
14. Bloom and Chatterji (2009).
15. Guclu, Dees, and Anderson (2004).
16. Austin and Porraz (2002).
17. Bloom (2009).
18. Bloom and Chatterji (2009).
19. Grossman, Wei-Skillern, and Lieb (2003).
20. Divine Chocolate (2009).
21. Big Issue (2009).
22. Housing Works (2009).
23. Rubicon Foundation (2009).
24. Community Wealth Ventures (2009).
25. Social Enterprise Reporter (2009).
26. Social Enterprise Alliance (2009).
27. Eakin (2003).
28. Wallace (1999).
29. Pearce (2003).
30. Borgaza and Defourny (2001).
31. M. Barker (personal communication, July 3, 2009).
32. R. McEwan (personal communication, June 25, 2009).
33. Tracey and Phillips (2007).

34. Cho (2006).

35. Parkinson and Howorth (2008).

36. R. Harding (personal communication, June 19, 2009).

37. Catalogue for Philanthropy (2000).

38. Leadbeater (1997).

39. Harding (2009).

40. Dees (1998b).

41. Dees and Anderson (2003); Austin, Leonard, Reficco, and Wei-Skillern (2004).

42. Austin, Stevenson, and Wei-Skillern (2006).

43. Korosec and Berman (2006).

44. Pomerantz (2003).

45. Dees (1998b).

46. Elkington (1994).

47. Thompson, Alvy, and Lees (2000).

48. Shokay (2009).

49. Pearce (2003); Bornstein (2004).

50. Dorado (2006).

51. Thompson, Alvy, and Lees (2000).

52. Austin, Stevenson, and Wei-Skillern (2006).

53. Theobald (1987).

54. R. Harding (personal communication, June 19, 2009).

55. Tracey and Phillips (2007).

56. Brinckerhoff (2000).

57. M. Barker (personal communication, July 3, 2009).

58. Tracey and Phillips (2007).

59. Greyston Bakery (2009a).

60. Dees (1998a).

61. Finn (2004).

62. Puttnam (2004).

63. Zadek and Thake (1997).

64. Bloom and Chatterji (2009).

65. Kiva (2009).

66. Charlton and May (1995).

67. Banuri and Najam (2002).

68. R. McEwan (personal communication, June 25, 2009).

69. Bradach and Tempest (2000).

70. Dees, Emerson, and Economy (2001).

71. Banuri, Najam, and Spanger-Siegfried (2003).

72. Bloom (2009).

73. Fowler (2000).

74. Pomerantz (2003).

75. Overholt, Dahle, and Canabou (2004).
76. Eikenberry and Kluver (2004).
77. Leadbeater (1997).
78. Bloom and Chatterji (2009).
79. Boyles (1997).
80. World of Good (2008); Mars and Garrison (2009).
81. Pomerantz (2003).
82. Mort, Weerawardena, and Carnegie (2003).
83. Cornwall (1998).
84. Tracey and Phillips (2007).
85. KickStart (2009).
86. Waddock and Post (1991).
87. Waddock and Post (1991).
88. Fowler (2000).
89. R. Harding (personal communication, June 19, 2009)
90. Pomerantz (2003).
91. Mort, Weerawardena, and Carnegie (2003).
92. Bloom (2009).
93. Harding (2004).
94. Tracey and Phillips (2007).
95. Wallace (1999).
96. Austin, Stevenson, and Wei-Skillern (2006).
97. Lissner (1977).
98. Harding and Harding (2008d).
99. Social Enterprise Alliance (2009).
100. Davis (1997).
101. Blackwood, Wing, and Pollak (2009).
102. Blackwood, Wing, and Pollak (2009).
103. Harding (2009).
104. Chu (2009).
105. Vilaga (2009c).
106. Rockwood (2009a).
107. Rockwood (2009b).
108. Anderson (2009a).
109. Vilaga (2009b).
110. Lee (2009).
111. Anderson (2009b).
112. Vilaga (2009a).
113. McGirt (2009).
114. Murray (2001).
115. Shore (2009).

Chapter 2

1. Jacob-Schanli and Murray (2001).
2. Finn (2004).
3. Harding and Harding (2008d).
4. M. Barker (personal communication, July 3, 2009).
5. Pomerantz (2003).
6. M. Barker (personal communication, July 3, 2009).
7. Fowler (2000).
8. KaBOOM (2009).
9. Wilken (1979).
10. R. Harding (personal communication, June 19, 2009).
11. Girls on the Run (2009).
12. Dees (1998b).
13. Social Enterprise Alliance (2009e).
14. KaBOOM (2009).
15. Puttnam (2004).
16. KickStart (2009).
17. Mort, Weerawardena, and Carnegie (2003).
18. Social Enterprise Alliance (2009j).
19. Social Enterprise Alliance (2009h).
20. Waddock and Post (1991).
21. Girls on the Run (2009).
22. M. Barker (personal communication, July 3, 2009).
23. Paton (2003).
24. Waddock and Post (1991).
25. Harding (2004).
26. Waddock and Post (1991).
27. Harding (2004).
28. Henton, Melville, and Walesh (1997).
29. Korosec and Berman (2006).
30. Hartigan (2006).
31. R. McEwan (personal communication, June 25, 2009).
32. Medbank (2009).
33. Leadbeater (1997).
34. R. McEwan (personal communication, June 25, 2009).
35. Trosa, Inc. (2009).
36. Kiva (2009).
37. Catford (1998).
38. Waddock and Post (1991)
39. Ten Thousand Villages (2009).
40. Catford (1998).
41. Henton, Melville, and Walesh (1997).

42. Waddock and Post (1991).

43. R. Harding (personal communication, June 19, 2009).

44. Leadbeater (1997).

45. Harding (2004).

46. R. McEwan (personal communication, June 25, 2009).

47. Harding and Harding (2008d).

48. KaBOOM (2009).

49. Department of Trade and Industry (2002).

50. YouthBuild (2009).

51. Leadbeater (1997).

52. Harding (2004).

53. Green-Works (2009).

54. R. McEwan (personal communication, July 3, 2009).

55. Reis and Clohesy (1999).

56. Henton, Melville, and Walesh (1997).

57. Hartigan (2006).

58. KickStart (2009).

59. KickStart (2009).

60. Kanter (1999).

61. Harding (2004).

62. Harding and Harding (2008d).

63. Boyles (1997).

64. Hartigan (2006).

65. Social Enterprise Alliance (2009k).

66. Falk (2000).

67. Scholte (2000).

68. Post (2000).

69. World Economic Forum (2002).

70. Berenbeim (2005).

71. Salamon (1993).

72. Elshtain (1999).

73. Jaffee (2001).

74. Feeney (1997).

75. Snyder (1999).

76. Maignan and Ferrell (2000).

77. Waddock (2001).

78. Habisch, Meister, and Schmidpeter (2001).

79. David (2000).

80. Philanthropic Initiative (2000).

81. World Economic Forum (2002).

82. Friedman (1970).

83. World Economic Forum (2002).

84. Pozorski (2000).
85. Locke (2002).
86. Gingold (2000).
87. Baron (2007).
88. Harding (2004).
89. Hartigan (2006).
90. Dees (1998b).
91. Dees (2001).
92. Salamon (1997).
93. Bornstein (2004).
94. National Foundation for Teaching Entrepreneurship (2009).
95. Korosec and Berman (2006).
96. Alexander, Nank, and Stivers (1999).
97. Bloom and Chatterji (2009).
98. Harding (2004).
99. Eikenberry and Kluver (2004).
100. Harding (2004).
101. Michael (2006).
102. Harding (2004).
103. Alvord, Brown, and Letts (2004).
104. Sullivan (2007).
105. Sullivan (2007).
106. Harding (2004).
107. Dees (2001).
108. Thaler and Sunstein (2008).
109. Bloom and Chatterji (2009).
110. Nike (2009).
111. KaBOOM (2009).
112. Dees, Anderson, and Wei-Skillern (2004).
113. Froelich (1999).
114. Thompson (2002).
115. Frederickson (1982).
116. Partners in Health (2009).
117. Dees (2001).
118. Zander (1993).
119. Harding and Harding (2008a).
120. Adams and Perlmutter (1991).
121. Young (2002).
122. Cornforth (2003).
123. Harding and Harding (2008c).
124. Harding and Harding (2008a).
125. KickStart (2009).

126. Salamon (1997).
127. Social Enterprise Alliance (2009a).
128. KickStart (2009).
129. Social Enterprise Alliance (2009k).
130. Harding (2004).
131. Alvord, Brown, and Letts (2004).
132. McLeod (1997).
133. Tuckman and Chang (2004).
134. KickStart (2009).
135. Greyston Bakery (2009b).
136. World of Good (2009).
137. Reis and Clohesy (1999).
138. Endeavor (2009).
139. Thompson (2002).
140. Kramden (2009).
141. Grant and Crutchfield (2007).
142. Backman and Smith (2000).
143. Austin (2000).
144. M. Barker (personal communication, July 3, 2009).
145. Berenbeim (2005).
146. Hartigan (2006).
147. Edelman (1977).
148. Teach for America (2009).
149. Hartigan (2006).
150. Bennis and Nanus (1985).
151. Partners in Health (2009).

Chapter 3

1. O'Hanlon (2001).
2. Whitelock and Munday (1993).
3. M. Barker (personal communication, July 3, 2009).
4. Eikenberry and Kluver (2004).
5. "It Takes a Village" (2009).
6. Johanson and Vahlne (1977).
7. Vahlne and Nordstrom (1993).
8. M. Barker (personal communication, July 3, 2009).
9. Banuri, Najam, and Spanger-Siegfried (2003).
10. Adelman and Morris (1997).
11. R. McEwan (personal communication, June 25, 2009).
12. Wellman (1999).
13. R. Harding (personal communication, June 19, 2009).

14. Norvell, Andrus, and Gmalla (1995).

15. Slater and Narver (1995).

16. Fowler (2000).

17. Granovetter (1973).

18. Fillis and McAuley (2000).

19. Mort, Weerawardena, and Carnegie (2003).

20. Manlova, Brush, Edelman, and Greene (2002).

21. Johanson and Vahlne (1990).

22. M. Barker (personal communication, July 3, 2009).

23. Johanson and Vahlne (1990).

24. d'Amboise and Muldowney (1988).

25. Reuber and Fischer (1997).

26. Grant (1987).

27. Buckley (1989).

28. O'Reilly, Snyder, and Boothe (1993).

29. M. Barker (personal communication, July 3, 2009).

30. Gilbert, McDougall, and Audretsch (2006).

31. Reynolds, Hay, Bygrave, Camp, and Autio (2000).

32. Roth (1992).

33. Mitchell, Shaver, and Yeung (1992).

34. R. McEwan (personal communication, June 25, 2009).

35. Mugler and Miesenbock (1986).

36. Wilson (2000).

37. Smallbone and Wyer (1995).

38. Aldrich and Auster (1986).

39. Reeb, Kwok, and Baek (1998).

40. Johanson and Vahlne (1977).

41. Madhok and Tallman (1998).

42. Petersen, Welch, and Welch (2000).

43. Chetty and Campbell-Hunt (2003).

44. Chetty and Campbell-Hunt (2004).

45. Shapiro (1986).

46. Servaes (1996).

47. R. Harding (personal communication, June 19, 2009).

48. Hitt, Hoskisson, and Ireland (1994).

49. Lu and Beamish (2004).

50. Zott (2003).

51. Weiss and Anderson (1992).

52. Benito, Pedersen, and Petersen (1999).

53. Lee and Kwok (1988).

54. Sapienza, Autio, George, and Zahra (2006).

55. R. Harding (personal communication, June 19, 2009).

56. Jensen (1986).

57. Johanson and Vahlne (1977).

58. Marschan-Piekkari, Welch, and Welch (1999).

59. R. McEwan (personal communication, June 25, 2009).

60. Monti and Yip (2000).

61. Burns (2009).

62. Geringer, Beamish, and duCosta (1989).

63. Pakes and Ericson (1998).

64. Acs, Arenius, Hay, and Minniti (2004).

65. Bloodgood, Sapienza, and Almeida (1996).

66. Bleyer, Gwinnel, Kamikawa, and Maurice (2009).

67. Marschan-Piekkari, Welch, and Welch (1999).

68. R. McEwan (personal communication, June 25, 2009).

69. Bleyer, Gwinnel, Kamikawa, and Maurice (2009).

70. Gilbert, McDougall, and Audretsch (2006).

71. Madhok and Tallman (1998).

72. Reeb, Kwok, and Baek (1998).

73. Chetty and Campbell-Hunt (2003).

74. M. Barker (personal communication, July 3, 2009).

75. Bhattacharya and Wheatley (2006).

76. Bae and Jain (2002).

77. Svetlicic, Jacklic, and Burger (2007).

78. Mitchell, Shaver, and Yeung (1992).

79. Wrigley and Currah (2003).

80. Datta, Rajagopalan, and Rasheed (1991).

81. Oviatt and McDougall (2005).

82. World of Good (2009).

83. Rugman (1981).

84. Bleyer, Gwinnel, Kamikawa, and Maurice (2009).

85. R. Harding (personal communication, June 19, 2009).

86. Datta, Rajagopalan, and Rasheed (1991).

87. M. Barker (personal communication, July 3, 2009).

88. Bleyer, Gwinnel, Kamikawa, and Maurice (2009); Community Wealth (2009).

89. Westhead, Wright, and Ucbarasan (2001).

90. Oviatt and McDougall (1994).

91. Bleyer, Gwinnel, Kamikawa, and Maurice (2009); Parker (2008).

92. Sapienza, Autio, George, and Zahra (2006).

93. Bleyer, Gwinnel, Kamikawa, and Maurice (2009).

94. Hamel and Prahalad (1985).

95. Hardy (1986).

96. Grant (1987).

97. Brush (1992).
98. Miller and Pras (1980).
99. Hitt, Hoskisson, and Ireland (1994).
100. Bleyer, Gwinnel, Kamikawa, and Maurice (2009).
101. Kwok and Reeb (2000).
102. KickStart (2009).
103. Knight and Cavusgil (1996).
104. Porter (1990).
105. Buhner (1987).
106. Elango (2000).
107. Social Enterprise Alliance (2009f).
108. Bleyer, Gwinnel, Kamikawa, and Maurice (2009); Reynolds (2008).
109. Hitt, Hoskisson, and Ireland (1994).
110. Bleyer, Gwinnel, Kamikawa, and Maurice (2009).
111. Goshal (1987).
112. Kwok and Reeb (2000).
113. Peng and Heath (1996).
114. Goshal (1987).
115. Friedman (2000).

Chapter 4

1. Murray (2001).
2. Social Enterprise Alliance (2009k).
3. Brinckerhoff (2000).
4. Anderson (2009a).
5. Harding and Harding (2008b).
6. Bloom and Chatterji (2009).
7. Thompson, Alvy, and Lees (2000).
8. Overholt, Dahle, and Canabou (2004).
9. Harding and Harding (2008c).
10. Fowler (2000).
11. Harding and Harding (2008b).
12. Dees (1998b).
13. National Foundation for Teaching Entrepreneurship (2009).
14. Fowler (2000).
15. Harding and Harding (2008a).
16. Waddock and Post (1991).
17. Dees (1998b).
18. Mort, Weerawardena, and Carnegie (2003).
19. Greve and Salaff (2003).
20. Harding (2009).

21. Harding and Harding (2008b).
22. Olson (1965).
23. Social Enterprise Alliance (2009h).
24. Waddock and Post (1991).
25. Carroll (1993).
26. Edelman (1977).
27. Bellah, Madsen, Sullivan, Swidler, and Tipton (1985).
28. Burns (1978).
29. M. Barker (personal communication, July 3, 2009).
30. Kingdon (1984).
31. Social Enterprise Alliance (2009g).
32. M. Barker (personal communication, July 3, 2009).
33. Social Enterprise Alliance (2009k).
34. R. Harding (personal communication, June 19, 2009).
35. Harding (2009).
36. Social Enterprise Alliance (2009d).
37. Social Enterprise Alliance (2009i).
38. Social Enterprise Alliance (2009i).
39. Social Enterprise Alliance (2009c).
40. Social Enterprise Alliance (2009b).
41. Social Enterprise Alliance (2009g).
42. R. Harding (personal interview, June 19, 2009).
43. Dees, Emerson, and Economy (2001).
44. Banuri, Najam, and Spanger-Siegfried (2003).

Chapter 5

1. Harding and Harding (2008b).
2. Bleyer, Gwinnel, Kamikawa, and Maurice (2009); International Franchise Organization (2009).
3. Social Enterprise Alliance (2009f).
4. Hartigan (2006).
5. Harding and Harding (2008b).
6. YouthBuild (2009).
7. Welch and Luostarinen (1988).
8. Elango (2004).
9. Boddewyn (1988).
10. Johanson and Vahlne (1990).
11. Dunning (1988).
12. Teece (1986).
13. Anderson and Gatignon (1986).
14. Cavusgil (1980).

15. Andersson (2000).

16. Brandes and Brege (1993).

17. Johanson and Vahlne (1990).

18. Jones (1999).

19. Andersson (2000).

20. Freeman and Cavusgil (2007).

21. Social Enterprise Alliance (2009h).

22. Fletcher and Bohn (1998).

23. Carpenter and Frederickson (2001).

24. Bilkey (1978).

25. Aharoni (1966).

26. Zahra and George (2002).

27. Child, Ng, and Wong (2002).

28. Brush and Vanderwerf (1992).

29. Wrigley and Currah (2003).

30. Arbaugh, Camp, and Cox (2008).

31. Kogut and Singh (1988).

32. Child, Ng, and Wong (2002).

33. Eriksson, Johanson, Majkgard, and Sharma (2000).

34. Wrigley and Currah (2003).

35. Hannan (1998).

36. Cuervo-Cazurra and Genc (2008).

37. Endeavor (2009).

38. Knight and Cavusgil (1996).

39. Autio, Sapienza, and Almeida (2000).

40. Social Enterprise Alliance (2009h).

41. Social Enterprise Alliance (2009k).

42. Social Enterprise Alliance (2009i).

43. Matthews (2006).

44. "It Takes a Village" (2009).

45. Kaynak and Kothani (1984).

46. Cavusgil (1976).

47. Carpenter and Frederickson (2001).

48. Hitt, Bierman, Uhlenbruck, and Shimizu (2006).

49. Chung (2001).

50. Tallman and Li (1996).

51. Kim (1997).

52. Carland, Hoy, Boulton, and Carland (1984).

53. Davidson, Delmar, and Wiklund (2002).

54. Jones (1999).

55. Denis and Depelteau (1985).

56. Johanson and Vahlne (1977).

57. Calof and Beamish (1995).

58. Hill, Hwang, and Kim (1990).

59. Kogut (1991).

60. Chetty and Campbell-Hunt (2004).

61. Autio, Sapienza, and Almeida (2000).

62. Goshal (1987).

63. Afuah (1998).

64. Lee and Park (2006).

65. Grant (1996).

66. Madhok (1997).

67. M. Barker (personal communication, July 3, 2009).

68. Barkema, Bell, and Pennings (1996).

69. Ellis (2000).

70. Kotha, Rindova, and Rothaermel (2001).

71. Plunley (2000).

72. Kim (1997).

73. Lechner and Dowling (2003).

74. Steensma, Marino, Weaver, and Dickson (2000).

75. Hitt, Lee, and Yucel (2002).

76. Hitt, Bierman, Uhlenbruck, and Shimizu (2006).

77. Axelsson and Johanson (1992).

78. Woolcock and Narayan (2000).

79. Kotha, Rindova, and Rothaermel (2001).

80. Hakanson (1982).

81. Wong and Ellis (2002).

82. Chang (1995).

83. Garcia-Canal, Lopez, Rialp, and Valde (2002).

84. Kogut and Singh (1988).

85. Social Enterprise Alliance (2009k).

86. Lecraw (1977).

87. Social Enterprise Alliance (2009k).

88. McGirt (2009).

89. McDougall (1989).

90. Coviello and Munro (1995).

91. Chetty and Campbell-Hunt (2004).

92. M. Barker (personal communication, July 3, 2009).

93. Johanson and Weidershiem-Paul (1975).

94. Hitt, Hoskisson, and Ireland (1994).

95. Rui and Yip (2008).

96. Hitt, Hoskisson, and Ireland (1994).

97. Caves (1982).

98. Brush (1992).

99. Porter (1985).
100. Social Enterprise Alliance (2009k).
101. Social Enterprise Alliance (2009c).
102. Hambrick and Mason (1984).
103. Harrigan (2001).
104. Kalantaridis (2004).
105. Social Enterprise Alliance (2009k).
106. Vermeulen (2001).
107. M. Barker (personal communication, July 3, 2009).
108. Caves (1996).
109. Child, Ng, and Wong (2002).
110. Chang (1995).
111. Caves (1982).
112. Rhyne (2005).
113. Julien, Joyal, Deshaies, and Ramangalahy (1997).
114. Prahalad and Hamel (1990).
115. Tallman and Fladmoe-Lindquist (2002).
116. Kim, Hwang, and Burgers (1993).
117. Hamel and Prahalad (1985).
118. KickStart (2009).
119. Meyer and Rowan (1977).
120. Social Enterprise Alliance (2009g).
121. Social Enterprise Alliance (2009h)
122. Svetlicic, Jacklic, and Burger (2007).
123. Rui and Yip (2008).
124. Brush and Vanderwerf (1992).
125. Eisenhardt and Martin (2000).
126. Prahalad and Hamel (1990).
127. Barham and Heimer (1998).
128. Social Enterprise Alliance (2009h).
129. M. Barker (personal communication, July 3, 2009).
130. Weisbrod (1998).
131. Endeavor (2009).

Chapter 6

1. Callan (2001).
2. M. Barker (personal communication, July 3, 2009).
3. Fowler (2000).
4. Social Enterprise Alliance (2009g).
5. Hartigan (2006).
6. Hirschman (1958).

7. Foley and Edwards (1995).

8. Fowler (2000).

9. Davis (1997).

10. Shore (2009).

11. Edwards, Hulme, and Wallace (1999).

12. Aldrich and Whetten (1981).

13. Bonbright (1997).

14. Waddock and Post (1991).

15. Madsen and Servais (1997).

16. Bleyer, Gwinnel, Kamikawa, and Maurice (2009).

17. Fowler (2000).

18. Caulkins (1980).

19. Burt (1992).

20. Hansen (1995).

21. Social Enterprise Alliance (2009g).

22. Larson (1992).

23. Freeman and Ruan (1997).

24. Renzulli, Aldrich, and Moody (2000).

25. Pomerantz (2003).

26. Mort, Weerawardena, and Carnegie (2003).

27. Social Enterprise Alliance (2009h).

28. Fowler (2000).

29. Gillingham, Ripley, and Nunez (2007).

30. Pomerantz (2003).

31. Overholt, Dahle, and Canabou (2004).

32. Burns (2009).

33. Davis (2002).

34. Paquet (1997).

35. Vilaga (2009a).

36. Leadbeater and Goss (1998).

37. McDougall (1991).

38. Papadopolous (1988).

39. Spreitzer, McCall, and Mahoney (1997).

40. Vermeulen (2001).

41. Chetty and Agndal (2007).

42. Hitt, Hoskisson, and Ireland (1994).

43. M. Barker (personal communication, July 3, 2009).

44. Prahalad and Hamel (1990).

45. Rockwood (2009b).

46. Hitt, Hoskisson, and Ireland (1994).

47. Social Enterprise Alliance (2009k).

48. Social Enterprise Alliance (2009h).

49. Social Enterprise Alliance (2009i).

50. Harding and Harding (2008b).

51. Matthews (2006).

52. Carpenter and Frederickson (2001).

53. Lee and Park (2006).

54. Barkema and Vermeulen (1998).

55. Vermeulen (2001).

56. Social Enterprise Alliance (2009k).

57. Vermeulen and Barkema (2001).

58. Caves (1982).

59. Hitt, Hoskisson, and Ireland (1994).

60. Harding and Harding (2008c).

61. M. Barker (personal communication, July 3, 2009).

62. Teece, Pisano, and Shuen (1997).

63. Wrigley and Currah (2003).

64. Hamel and Prahalad (1985).

65. Zhao and Luo (2002).

66. World of Good (2009).

67. Chang (1995).

68. Caves (1982).

69. Hamel and Prahalad (1985).

70. Oviatt and McDougall (1994).

71. Kim, Hwang, and Burgers (1993).

72. KickStart (2009).

73. Hamel and Prahalad (1985).

74. M. Barker (personal communication, July 3, 2009).

75. Casson (1992).

76. Hitt, Hoskisson, and Kim (1997).

77. Guillen and Garcia-Canal (2009).

78. Guillen and Garcia-Canal (2009).

79. Johanson and Weidershiem-Paul (1975).

80. Oviatt and McDougall (1994).

81. Johanson and Vahlne (1990).

82. Vermeulen (2001).

83. Social Enterprise Alliance (2009k).

84. KickStart (2009).

85. Shane (1994).

86. Barkema, Bell, and Pennings (1996).

87. Sarkar, Cavusgil, and Aulakh (1999).

88. Forsgren (1990).

89. Rui and Yip (2008).

90. Vermeulen (2001).

91. Gomes-Casseres (1996).

92. Garcia-Canal, Lopez, Rialp, and Valde (2002).

93. Dunning (1993).

94. Vernon (1966).

95. Porter (1990).

96. Doole and Lowe (1999).

97. Social Enterprise Alliance (2009f).

98. Shore (2009).

99. National Foundation for Teaching Entrepreneurship (2009).

100. Antoncic and Hisrich (2000).

101. McDougall (1989).

102. Zahra, Ireland, Gutierrez, and Hitt (2000).

103. Jones (1999).

104. Coviello and Munro (1995).

105. Anderson (2009b).

106. Kogut and Singh (1988).

107. Chang (1995).

108. Kuemmerle (2002).

109. Social Enterprise Alliance (2009k).

110. Denis and Depelteau (1985).

111. Cohen and Levinthal (1990).

112. Calof and Beamish (1995).

113. Barkema, Bell, and Pennings (1996).

114. Afuah (1998).

115. Goshal (1987).

116. Sanders and Carpenter (1998).

117. Grant (1996).

118. Cortright (2006).

119. Brush and Vanderwerf (1992).

120. Johanson and Vahlne (1977).

121. Endeavor (2009).

122. Hitt, Hoskisson, and Ireland (1994).

123. R. Harding (personal communication, June 19, 2009).

124. Elango (2006).

125. M. Barker (personal communication, July 3, 2009).

126. Plunley (2000).

127. Harrigan (2001).

128. Kalantaridis (2004).

129. Terjesen, O'Gorman, and Acs (2008).

130. Endeavor (2009).

131. Hambrick and Mason (1984).

132. Lecraw (1977).

133. Social Enterprise Alliance (2009f).
134. R. McEwan (personal communication, June 25, 2009).
135. M. Barker (personal communication, July 3, 2009).
136. Hitt, Lee, and Yucel (2002).
137. Hitt, Bierman, Uhlenbruck, and Shimizu (2006).
138. Chin-Chun (2006).
139. Sanders and Carpenter (1998).
140. Lee and Park (2006).
141. Endeavor (2009).
142. Pronk (2002).

Chapter 7

1. Jacob-Scharli (2001).
2. Korosec and Berman (2006).
3. Cummins, Gilmore, Carson, and O'Donnell (2000).
4. Jolly, Alahuhta, and Jeannet (1992).
5. Prahalad and Hart (2002).
6. "Banking on the Poor" (1998).
7. Ashoka (2004).
8. Cox and Healy (1998).
9. Boris and Steuerel (1999).
10. R. Harding (personal communication, June 19, 2009).
11. Bradach (2003).
12. R. Harding (personal communication, June 19, 2009).
13. Letts, Grossman, and Ryan (1999).
14. Young and Salamon (2002).
15. Tuckman and Chang (2004).
16. Boschee (2001).
17. Pharoah, Scott, and Fisher (2004).
18. Foster and Bradach (2005).
19. Waddock and Post (1991).
20. Dees, Anderson, and Wei-Skillern (2004).
21. Grossman, Wei-Skillern, and Lieb (2003).
22. Social Enterprise Alliance (2009b).
23. Burns (2009).
24. Oster (1995).
25. Anderson (2009).
26. Letts, Grossman, and Ryan (1999).
27. Social Enterprise Alliance (2009k).
28. R. McEwan (personal communication, June 25, 2009).
29. Austin, Stevenson, and Wei-Skillern (2006).
30. R. McEwan (personal communication, June 25, 2009).

31. Pharoah, Scott, and Fisher (2004).
32. Pharoah, Scott, and Fisher (2004).
33. Bloom and Chatterji (2009).
34. Waddock and Post (1991).
35. Austin, Stevenson, and Wei-Skillern (2006).
36. Social Enterprise Alliance (2009).
37. Light (2008).
38. Korosec and Berman (2006).
39. Bloom and Chatterji (2009).
40. Fowler (2000).
41. R. Harding (personal communication, June 19, 2009).
42. Theobald (1987).
43. Banuri, Najam, and Spanger-Siegfried (2003).
44. Tyson (2004).
45. Banuri and Najam (2002).
46. Adelman and Morris (1997).
47. Beamish, Morrison, Rosenzweig, and Inkpen (2000).
48. Fowler (2000).
49. Karakaya and Stahl (1991).
50. Bridges.org (2002).
51. Puttnam (2004).
52. Fowler (2000).
53. Leadbeater and Goss (1998).
54. Anderson and Gatignon (1986).
55. Fowler (2000).
56. Suchman (1995).
57. Puttnam (2004).
58. Jenssen and Koenig (2002).
59. Davis (2002).
60. Kotler and Armstrong (1999).
61. Mort, Weerawardena, and Carnegie (2003).

Chapter 8

1. Frank (2007).
2. R. Harding (personal communication, June 19, 2009).
3. Harding and Harding (2008d).
4. R. Harding (personal communication, June 19, 2009).
5. Rogerson (2004).
6. Svetlicic, Jacklic, and Burger (2007).
7. R. McEwan (personal communication, June 25, 2009).
8. Dees (1998b).
9. Chetty and Agndal (2007).

10. Tallman and Li (1996).

11. Vermeulen (2001).

12. Aldrich and Whetten (1981).

13. Hansmann (1987).

14. Thompson, Alvy, and Lees (2000).

15. Fillis (2000).

16. Puttnam (2004).

17. Madsen and Servais (1997).

18. R. Harding (personal communication, June 19, 2009).

19. Harding and Harding (2008d).

20. Norvell, Andrus, Deine, and Gogumalla (1988).

21. Anderson and Gatignon (1986).

22. Austin, Stevenson, and Wei-Skillern (2006).

23. Uzzi (1997).

24. Puttnam (2004).

25. Hart (1984).

26. Waddock and Post (1991).

27. Korosec and Berman (2006).

28. Herman and Redina (2001).

29. Young (1997).

30. Herbst (2004).

31. Pomerantz (2003).

32. Mort, Weerawardena, and Carnegie (2003).

33. Thompson, Alvy, and Lees (2000).

34. Brinckerhoff (2000).

35. Leadbeater and Goss.

36. Paquet (1997).

37. Pomerantz (2003).

38. Bloom and Chatterji (2009).

39. R. McEwan (personal communication, June 25, 2009).

40. Harding and Harding (2008d).

41. Tracey and Phillips (2007).

42. Jones and English (2004).

43. Tracey and Phillips (2007).

44. Mars and Garrison (2009).

45. Tracey and Phillips (2007).

46. Mars and Garrison (2009).

47. Harding (2009).

48. R. McEwan (personal communication, June 25, 2009).

49. R. McEwan (personal communication, June 25, 2009).

50. R. McEwan (personal communication, June 25, 2009).

51. Shore (2009).

References

Acs, Z. J., Arenius, P., Hay, M., & Minniti, M. (2004). *Global entrepreneurship monitor: 2004 executive report.* Wellesley, MA: Babson College and London Business School.

Adams, C., & Perlmutter, F. (1991). Commercial venturing and the transformation of America's voluntary social welfare agencies. *Nonprofit and Voluntary Sector Quarterly, 20*(1), 25–38.

Adelman, I., & Morris, C. (1997). Development history and its implications for development theory. *World Development, 25*(6), 831–840.

Afuah, A. (1998). *Innovation management: Strategies, implementation, and profits.* New York: Oxford University Press.

Aharoni, Y. (1966). *The foreign investment decision process.* Boston, MA: Division of Research, Graduate School of Business Administration, Harvard University.

Aldrich, H. E., & Auster, E. (1986). Even dwarfs started small: Liabilities of size and age and their strategic implications. *Research in Organizational Behavior, 8*(1), 165–198.

Aldrich, H. E., & Whetten, D. A. (1981). Organization sets, action sets, and networks: Making the most of simplicity. In P. Nystrom and W. Starbuck (Eds.), *Handbook of organizational design I.* London, England: Oxford University Press.

Alexander, J., Nank, R., & Stivers, C. (1999). Implications of welfare reform: Do nonprofit survival strategies threaten civil society? *Nonprofit and Voluntary Sector Quarterly, 28*(4), 452–475.

Alvord, S. H., Brown, L. D., & Letts, C. W. (2004). Social entrepreneurship and societal transformation: An exploratory study. *Journal of Applied Behavioral Science, 40,* 262–282.

Anderson, S. (2009a). *Civic ventures.* Retrieved from http://www.fastcompany .com/magazine/131/civic-ventures-silicon-valley-encore-initiative.html

Anderson, S. (2009b). *Husk power systems.* Retrieved from http://www.fastcompany .com/magazine/131/husk-power-systems-rice-fired-electricity.html

Andersson, S. (2000). The internationalization of the firm from an entrepreneurial perspective. *International Studies of Management & Organization, 30*(1), 3–92.

Anderson, E., & Gatignon, H. (1986). Modes of foreign entry: A transaction cost analysis and propositions. *Journal of International Business Studies, 17*(3), 1–26.

Anonymous. (2004). *Wearmouth community development trust.* Retrieved March 27, 2010, from http://www.se-alliance.org/case_studies/4_2004b.pdf

Anonymous (2005). *Lessons from PTBA*. Retrieved March 27, 2010, from http://www.se-alliance.org/case_studies/5_2005.pdf

Anonymous. (2009a). *About housing works*. Retrieved July 12, 2009, from http://www.housingworks.org/about

Anonymous. (2009b). *About Rubicon Foundation*. Retrieved July 12, 2009, from http://rubicon-foundation.org/

Anonymous. (2009c). *About Social Alliance Enterprise*. Retrieved July 12, 2009, from http://se-alliance.org/about_us.cfm

Anonymous. (2009d). *Social entrepreneurship profile—Wearmouth Community Development Trust Case (PTBA)*. Retrieved July 12, 2009, from http://www.se-alliance.org/case_studies/4_2004b.pdf

Antoncic, B., & Hisrich, R. D. (2000). An integrative conceptual model. *Journal of Euromarketing, 9*, 17–35.

Arbaugh, J. B., Camp, S. M., & Cox, L. W. (2008). Why don't entrepreneurial firms internationalize more? *Journal of Management Issues, 20*(3), 366–382.

Ashoka Foundation. (2004). *Ashoka's mission*. Retrieved from http://www.ashoka.org.za

Austin, J. E. (2000). *The collaboration challenge: How nonprofits and business succeed through strategic alliances*. San Francisco, CA: Jossey-Bass.

Austin, J. E., Leonard, H., Reficco, E., & Wei-Skillern, J. (2004). *Corporate social entrepreneurship: A new vision of CSR*. Harvard Business School Working Paper No. 05-021. Boston, MA: Harvard Business School.

Austin, J. E., & Porraz, J. M. (2002). *KaBOOM!* HBS Case No. 9-303-025. Boston, MA: Harvard Business School.

Austin, J., Stevenson, H., & Wei-Skillern, J. (2006). Social and commercial entrepreneurship: Same, different, or both? *Entrepreneurship: Theory & Practice, 30*(1), 1–22.

Autio, E., Sapienza, H., & Almeida, J. (2000). Effects of age at entry, knowledge intensity, and imitability on international growth. *Academy of Management Journal, 43*(5), 902–906.

Axelsson, B., & Johanson, J. (1992). Foreign market entry: The textbook vs. the network view. In B. Axelsson & G. Easton (Eds.), *Industrial networks: A new study of reality* (pp. 218–234). London, England: Routledge.

Backman, E. V., & Smith, S. R. (2000). Healthy organizations, unhealthy communities? *Nonprofit Management and Leadership, 10*(4), 355–373.

Bae, C. S., & Jain, V. (2002). *Multinationality: Evidence from U.S. industrial firms*. Paper presented at the Academy of International Business Meeting, San Juan, Puerto Rico.

Banking on the poor. (1998). *The Times*. Retrieved June 25, 2009, from http://www.grameen-info.org/agrameen/article.php3?article=3

Banuri, T., & Najam, A. (2002). *A civil society perspective on sustainable development*. Retrieved from http://humandevelopment.bu.edu/papers/civic_entrepreneurship.pdf

Banuri, T., Najam, A., & Spanger-Siegfried, E. (2003). *Civic entrepreneurship: In search of sustainable development*. Retrieved from http://www.iied.org/docs/global_gov/sd_opinion2.pdf

Barham, K., & Heimer, C. (1998). *ABB: The dancing giant—Creating the globally connected corporation*. London, England: Financial Times and Pittman.

Barkema, H. G., Bell, J. H., & Pennings, J. M. (1996). Foreign entry, cultural barriers, and learning. *Strategic Management Journal, 17*(2), 151–166.

Barkema, H. G., & Vermeulen, F. (1998). International expansion through start-up or acquisition: A learning perspective. *Academy of Management Journal, 41*, 7–26.

Baron, D. (2007). Corporate social responsibility and social entrepreneurship. *Journal of Economics & Management Strategy, 16*(3), 683–717.

Bartlett, C., & Ghoshal, S. (1998). *Managing across borders* (2nd ed.). Boston, MA: Harvard Business School.

Beamish, P. W., Morrison, A. J., Rosenzweig, P. M., & Inkpen, A. (2000). *International management: Text and cases*. Boston, MA: McGraw-Hill.

Bellah, R. N., Madsen, R., Sullivan, W. M., Swidler, A., & Tipton, S. M. (1985). *Habits of the heart: Individualism and commitment in American life*. New York: Harper & Row.

Benito, G. R. G., Pedersen, T., & Petersen, B. (1999). Foreign operation methods and switching costs: Conceptual issues and possible effects. *Scandinavian Journal of Management, 15*(2), 213–229.

Bennis, W., & Nanus, B. (1985). *Leaders: The strategies for taking charge*. New York: Harper & Row.

Berenbeim, R. (2005). The value based enterprise: A new corporate citizenship paradigm. *Executive Speeches, 19*(4), 7–1.

Bhattacharya, M., & Wheatley, K. K. (2006). Organizational risk and capital investments: A longitudinal examination of performance effects and moderating contexts. *Journal of Management Issues, 18*(1), 62–83.

Big Issue. (2009). *About Big Issue*. Retrieved from http://www.bigissue.com

Bilkey, W. J. (1978). An attempted integration of the literature on the export behavior of firms. *Journal of International Business Studies, 9*(1), 33–46.

Blackwood, A., Wing, K., & Pollak, J. (2009). *The nonprofit sector in brief*. Retrieved from http://nccsdataweb.urban.org/kbfiles/797/Almanac2008publicCharities.pdf

Bleyer, S., Gwinnel, D., Kamikawa, M., & Maurice, E. (2009). *International social franchising: A pathway for independence for INGOs*. Retrieved from http://

www.communitywealth.com/CWV%20Capstone%20Team%20Findings %20Report%20--FINAL%20--%2024%20Apr%2009.pdf

Bloodgood, J., Sapienza, H., & Almeida, J. (1996). The internationalization of new high-potential U.S. ventures: Antecedents and outcomes. *Entrepreneurship Theory & Practice, 20,* 61–76.

Bloom, P. N. (2009). Overcoming consumption constraints through social entrepreneurship. *Journal of Public Policy & Marketing, 28*(1), 128–134.

Bloom, P. N., & Chatterji, A. K. (2009). Scaling social entrepreneurial impact. *California Management Review, 51*(3), 114–133.

Boddewyn, J. J. (1988). Political aspects of MNE theory. *Journal of International Business Studies, 19*(3), 341–363.

Bonbright, D. (1997). *Leading public entrepreneurs.* San Francisco, CA: Ashoka Foundation.

Borgaza, C., & Defourny, J. (2001). *The emergence of social enterprise.* London, England: Routledge.

Boris, E., & Steuerel, E. (1999). *Nonprofits and government: Collaboration and conflict.* Washington, DC: Urban Institute Press.

Bornstein, D. (2004). *How to change the world: Social entrepreneurs and the power of new ideas.* New York: Oxford University Press.

Boschee, J. (2001). Eight basic principles for nonprofit entrepreneurs. *Nonprofit World, 19*(4), 15–18.

Botman, H. R. (2004). *The oikos in a global economic era.* Retrieved from http:// www.crvp.org/book/Series02/II-6/chapter_x.htm

Boyles, A. (1997). The rise of civil society. *One Country,* (2), 25–36.

Bradach, J. L. (2003). Going to scale. *Stanford Social Innovation Review, 1,* 18–25.

Bradach, J. L., & Tempest, N. (2000). *New schools venture fund.* HBS Case No. 9-301-038. Boston, MA: Harvard Business School.

Brandes, O., & Brege, S. (1993). The successful double turnaround of ASEA and ABB. *Journal of Strategic Change, 2,* 185–207.

Bridges.org. (2002). *Supporting entrepreneurship in developing countries: Survey of the field and inventory of initiatives.* Retrieved from http://www.bridges.org/ entrepreneurship/entrepreneurship_inventory.pdf

Brinckerhoff, P. C. (2000). *Social entrepreneurship: The art of mission-based venture development.* New York: John Wiley & Sons.

Brush, C. (1992). *Factors motivating small firms to internationalize: The effect of firm age* (Unpublished doctoral dissertation). Boston University, Boston.

Brush, C. G., & Vanderwerf, P. A. (1992). A comparison of methods and sources for obtaining estimates of new venture performance. *Journal of Business Venturing, 7,* 157–170.

Buckley, P.J. (1989). Foreign investment by small and medium sized enterprises: The theoretical background. *Small Business Economics, 1*(1), 89–100.

Buhner, R. (1987). Assessing international diversification of West German corporations. *Strategic Management Journal, 8,* 25–37.

Burns, J. M. (1978). *Leadership.* New York: Harper & Row.

Burns, M. (2009). *How to create jobs, save the planet, and make money for your non-profit (BWB).* Retrieved March 26, 2010, from http://www.se-alliance .org/case_studies/create_jobs.pdf

Burt, R. S. (1992). *Structural holes: The social structure of competition.* Cambridge, MA: Harvard University Press.

Callan, E. (2001). *Wenceslao Casares: Keen weather eye steers to safety.* Retrieved from http://specials.ft.com/davos2001/FT3MXR3CAIC.html

Calof, J. L., & Beamish, P. W. (1995). Adapting to foreign markets: Explaining internationalization. *International Business Review, 4*(2), 115–131.

Carland, J. W., Hoy, F., Boulton, W. R., & Carland, J. C. (1984). Differentiating entrepreneurship from small business owners: A conceptualization. *Academy of Management Review, 9,* 354–359.

Carpenter, M. A., & Frederickson, J. W. (2001). Top management teams, global strategic posture, and moderating role of uncertainty. *Academy of Management Journal, 44,* 533–545.

Carroll, A. (1993). *Business and society: Ethics and stakeholder management.* Cincinnati, OH: South Western Publishing.

Casson, M. (1992). Internalisation theory and beyond. In P. J. Buckley (Ed.), *New directions in international business: Research priorities for the 1990s* (pp. 4–27). Aldershot: Edward Elgar.

Catalogue for Philanthropy. (2000). *The Massachusetts catalogue for philanthropy.* Boston, MA: Ellis L. Phillips Foundation.

Catford, J. (1998). Social entrepreneurs are vital for health promotion—but they need supportive environments too. *Health Promotion International, 13*(2), 95–97.

Caulkins, D. (1980). Community, subculture, and organizational networks in Western Norway. *Journal of Voluntary Action Research, 9*(14), 35–44.

Caves, R. R. (1982). *Multinational enterprise and economic analysis.* Cambridge, England: Cambridge University Press.

Caves, R. R. (1996). *Multinational enterprise and economic analysis* (2nd ed.). Cambridge, England: Cambridge University Press.

Cavusgil, S. T. (1976). *Organizational determinants of firms' export behavior: An empirical analysis* (Unpublished doctoral dissertation). University of Wisconsin, Madison.

Cavusgil, S. T. (1980). On the internationalization process of firms. *European Research, 8,* 273–281.

Chang, S. J. (1995). International expansion strategy of Japanese firms: Capability building through sequential entry. *Academy of Management Journal, 38,* 383–407.

Charlton, R., & May, R. (1995). NGOs, politics, projects and probity: A policy implementation perspective. *Third World Quarterly, 16*(2), 237–255.

Chetty, S., & Agndal, H. (2007). Social capital and its influence on changes in internationalization mode among small and medium sized enterprises. *Journal of International Marketing, 1*(1), 1–29.

Chetty, S., & Campbell-Hunt, C. (2003). Explosive international growth and problems of success amongst small and medium-sized firms. *International Small Business Journal, 21*(1), 5–27.

Chetty, S., & Campbell-Hunt, C. (2004). A strategic approach to internationalization: A traditional versus a "born-global" approach. *Journal of International Marketing, 12*(1), 57–81.

Child, J., Ng, S. H., & Wong, C. (2002). Psychic distance and internationalization: Evidence from Hong Kong firms. *International Studies of Management & Organization, 32*(1), 36–56.

Chin-Chun, H. (2006). Internationalization and performance: The s-curve hypothesis and product diversity effect. *Multinational Business Review, 14*(2), 29–46.

Cho, A. H. (2006). *Politics, values and social entrepreneurship: A critical appraisal.* In Mair, J., Robinson, J., & Hockerts, K. (Eds.), *Social Entrepreneurship.* Basingstoke, England: Palgrave Macmillan.

Chu, J. (2009). *Do something.* Retrieved from http://www.fastcompany.com/magazine/131/do-something-an-ipo.html

Chung, W. (2001). Identifying technology transfer in foreign direct investment: Influence of industry conditions and investment firm motives. *Journal of International Business Studies, 32,* 211–230.

Cohen, W. M., & Levinthal, D. A. (1990). Absorptive capacity: A new perspective on learning and innovation. *Administrative Science Quarterly, 35,* 128–152.

Community Wealth Ventures. (2009a). *Streams of hope: Social franchising a new path to wealth for non-profits.* Retrieved from http://www.communitywealth.com/Streams%20of%20Hope.pdf

Community Wealth Ventures. (2009b). *About Community Wealth Ventures.* Retrieved from http://www.communitywealth.com

Cornforth, C. (2003). *The governance of public and nonprofit organizations: What do boards do?* London, England: Routledge.

Cornwall, J. (1998). The entrepreneur as building block for community. *Journal of Developmental Entrepreneurship, 3*(2), 141–148.

Cortright, J. (2006). *Making sense of clusters: Regional competitiveness and economic development*. Discussion paper. Washington, DC: The Brookings Institute in Metropolitan Policy Program.

Coviello, N. E., & Munro, H. (1995). Growing the entrepreneurial firm. *European Journal of Marketing, 29*(7), 49–61.

Cox, A., & Healy J. (1998). *Promises to the poor: The record of European development agencies. Poverty Briefing, 1*. London, England: Overseas Development Institute.

Cuervo-Cazurra, A., & Genc, M. (2008). Transforming disadvantages into advantages: Developing country MNEs in the least developed countries. *Journal of International Business Studies, 39*, 957–979.

Cummins, D., Gilmore, A., Carson, D., & O'Donnell, A. (2000). Innovative marketing in SMEs: A conceptual and descriptive framework. *New Product Development and Innovation Management, 8*(2), 231–248.

d'Amboise, G., & Muldowney, M. (1988). Management theory for small businesses: Attempts and requirements. *Academy of Management Review, 13*(2), 226–240.

Datta, D. K., Rajagopalan, N., & Rasheed, M. A. (1991). Diversification and performance: Critical review and future directions. *Journal of Management Studies, 28*, 529–548.

David, R. (2000). *Business in the community: BITC awards year 2000*. London, England: Financial Times.

Davidson, P., Delmar, F., & Wiklund, J. (2002). Entrepreneurship as growth: Growth as entrepreneurship. In M. A. Hitt, R. D. Ireland, S. M. Camp, & D. L. Sexton (Eds.), *Entrepreneurship: Creating a new mindset* (pp. 328–342). Oxford, England: Blackwell.

Davis, L. (1997). *The NGO business hybrid: Is private sector the answer*. Baltimore, MD: The John Hopkins University Press.

Davis, S. (2002). Social entrepreneurship: Towards an entrepreneurial culture for social and economic development. Retrieved from http://www.ashoka.org/global/yespaper.pdf

Dees, J. G. (1998a). Enterprising nonprofits. *Harvard Business Review, 76*(1), 54–67.

Dees, J. G. (1998b). *The meaning of "social entrepreneurship."* Retrieved from http://faculty.fuqua.duke.edu/centers/case/files/dees-SE.pdf

Dees, J. G. (2001). *The meaning of social entrepreneurship*. Working paper, Fuqua School of Business, Duke University, Durham, NC.

Dees, J. G., & Anderson, B. B. (2003). For-profit social ventures [Special issue]. *International Journal of Entrepreneurship Education, 2*, 1–26.

Dees, J. G., Anderson, B. B., & Wei-Skillern, J. (2004). Scaling social impact. *Stanford Social Innovation Review, 1*, 24–32.

Dees, J. G., Emerson, J., & Economy, P. (2001). *Enterprising nonprofits: A toolkit for social entrepreneurs.* New York: John Wiley.

Denis, J. E., & Depelteau, D. (1985). Market knowledge, diversification, and export expansion. *Journal of International Business Studies, 16*(3), 77–89.

Department of Trade and Industry. (2002). *Social enterprise: A strategy for success.* London, England: Department of Trade and Industry.

Divine Chocolate. (2009). *About Divine Chocolate.* Retrieved from http://www.divinechocolate.com/about/default.aspx

Doole, I., & Lowe, R. (1999). *International marketing strategy.* London, England: Thomson Learning.

Dorado, S. (2006). Social entrepreneurial ventures: Different values so different process of creation, no? *Journal of Developmental Entrepreneurship, 11*(4), 319–343.

Dunning, J. H. (1988). The eclectic paradigm of international production: A restatement and possible extension. *Journal of International Business Studies, 19*(1), 1–31.

Dunning, J. H. (1993). *Multinational enterprises and the global economy.* Workingham, England: Addison-Wesley.

Eakin, E. (2003, December 20). *How to save the world? Treat it like a business. New York Times,* p. 7.

Edelman, M. (1977). *Political language: Words that succeed and policies that fail.* New York: Academic Press.

Edwards, M., Hulme, D., & Wallace, T. (1999). NGOs in a global future: Marrying local delivery to worldwide leverage. *Public Administration and Development, 19*(2), 117–136.

Eikenberry, A., & Kluver, J. D. (2004). The marketization of the non-profit sector: Civil society at risk? *Public Administration Review, 64*(2), 132–140.

Eisenhardt, K., & Martin, J. (2000). Dynamic capabilities: What are they? *Strategic Management Journal, 2,* 1105–1121.

Elango, B. (2000). An exploratory study into the linkages between corporate resources and the extent and form of internationalization. *American Business Review, 18,* 12–26.

Elango, B. (2004). Geographic scope of operations by multinational companies: An exploratory study of regional and global strategies. *European Management Journal, 22,* 431–441.

Elango, B. (2006). An empirical analysis of the internationalization performance relationship across emerging market firms. *Multinational Business Review, 14*(1), 21–44.

Elkington, J. (1994). Towards the sustainable corporation: Win-win-win business strategies for sustainable development. *California Management Review, 36*(2), 90–100.

Ellis, P. (2000). Social ties and foreign market entry. *Journal of International Business Studies, 31*(3), 443–470.

Elshtain, J. B. (1999). A call to civil society. *Society, 36*(5), 11–19.

Endeavor. (2009). About Endeavor. Retrieved from http://www.endeavor.org

Eriksson, K., Johanson, J., Majkgard, A., & Sharma, D. (2000). Effect of variation on knowledge accumulation in the internationalization process. *International Studies of Management & Organization, 30*(1), 26–44.

Falk, R. (2000). The decline of citizenship in an era of globalization. *Citizenship Studies, 4*, 15–17.

Feeney, S. (1997). Shifting the prism: Case explications of institutional analysis in nonprofit organization. *Nonprofit and Voluntary Sector Quarterly, 26*(4), 489–508.

Fillis, I. (2000). Being creative at the marketing/entrepreneurship interface: Lessons from the art industry. *Journal of Research in Marketing and Entrepreneurship, 2*(2), 125–137.

Fillis, I., & McAuley, A. (2000). Modeling and measuring creativity at the interface. *Journal of Marketing Theory and Practice, 8*(2), 8–17.

Finn, W. (2004). Soul traders. *Director, 57*(7), 58–62.

Fletcher, R., & Bohn, J. (1998). The impact of psychic distance on the internationalization of the Australian firm. *Journal of Global Marketing, 12*(2), 47–68.

Foley, M., & Edwards, B. (1995). The paradox of civil society. *Journal of Democracy, 6*, 38.

Forsgren, M. (1990). Managing the international multi-center firm: Case studies from Sweden. *European Management Journal, 8*(2), 261–267.

Foster, W., & Bradach, J. (2005). Should nonprofits seek profits? *Harvard Business Review, 83*, 92–100.

Fowler, A. (2000). NGDOS as a moment in history: Beyond aid to social entrepreneurship or civic innovation? *Third World Quarterly, 21*(4), 637–654.

Frank, R. (2007). *Richistan: A journey through the American wealth boom and the lives of the new rich.* New York: Three Rivers.

Frederickson, H. G. (1982). The recovery of civicism in public administration. *Public Administration Review, 42*(6), 501–508.

Freeman, L. C., & Ruan, D. (1997). An international comparative study of interpersonal behavior and role relationships. *L'Annee sociologigue, 47*, 89–115.

Freeman, S., & Cavusgil, T. (2007). Toward a typology of commitment states among managers of born-global firms: A study of accelerated internationalization. *Journal of International Marketing, 15*(4), 1–40.

Friedman, M. (1970). The social responsibility of business is to increase its profits. *New York Times Magazine, 33*, 122–126.

Friedman, T. L. (2000). *The Lexus and the olive tree.* New York: Anchor Books.

Friedman, T. L. (2005). *The world is flat*. New York: Farrar, Straus & Giroux.

Froelich, K. (1999). Diversification of revenue strategies: Evolving resource dependence in non-profit organizations. *Non-profit and Voluntary Sector Quarterly, 28*, 246–268.

Garcia-Canal, E., Lopez, D., Rialp, C., & Valde, S. L. (2002). Accelerating international expansion through global alliances: A typology of cooperative strategies. *Journal of World Business, 37*(2), 91–107.

Geringer, J. M., Beamish, P. W., & duCosta, R. C. (1989). Diversification strategy and internationalization: Implications for MNE performance. *Strategic Management Journal, 10*, 109–119.

Gilbert, B. A., McDougall, P. P., & Audretsch, D. B. (2006). New venture growth: A review and extension. *Journal of Management, 32*, 926–950.

Gillingham, J., Ripley, C., & Nunez, M. (2007). *S.A.F.E. final business plan*. Tucson, AZ: University of Arizona, McGuire Center for Entrepreneurship.

Girls on the Run. (2009). *About Girls on the Run*. Retrieved from http://www.girlsontherun.org/default.html

Gingold, D. (2000). *New frontiers in philanthropy*. Retrieved from http://www.timeinc.net/fortune/sections

Gomes-Casseres, B. (1996). *The alliance revolution: The new shape of business rivalry*. Cambridge, MA: Harvard University Press.

Goshal, S. (1987). Global strategy: An organizing framework. *Strategic Management Journal 8*, 425–440.

Grameeninfo.org. (2010). *Introduction*. Retrieved March 26, 2010, from http://www.grameen-info.org/index.php?option=com_content&task=view&id=210&Itemid=379

Granovetter, M. (1973). The strength of weak ties. *American Journal of Sociology, 78*(6), 1360–1380.

Grant, H. M., & Crutchfield, L. R. (2007). Creating high impact nonprofits. *Stanford Social Innovation Review, 5*(3), 32–41.

Grant, R. M. (1987). Multinationality and performance among British manufacturing companies. *Journal of International Business Studies, 18*(3), 79–89.

Grant, R. M. (1996). Prospering in dynamically-competitive environments: Organizational capability as knowledge integration. *Organization Science, 7*, 375–387.

Greenberg, J., & Baron, R. A. (1997). *Behavior in organizations*. London, England: Prentice Hall.

Green-Works. (2009). *About Green-Works*. Retrieved from http://www.green-works.co.uk

Greve, A., & Salaff, J. W. (2003). Social networks and entrepreneurship. *Entrepreneurship Theory and Practice, 28*(1), 1–22.

Greyston Bakery. (2009a). *About Greyston Bakery*. Retrieved from http://www.greystonbakery.com

Greyston Bakery. (2009b). *Greyston Bakery guiding principles.* Retrieved from http://www.greystonbakery.com/guidingprinciples.php

Grossman, A., Wei-Skillern, J., & Lieb, K. J. (2003). *Guide dogs for the Blind Association.* HBS Case No. 9-303-006. Boston, MA: Harvard Business School.

Guclu, A. J., Dees, G., & Anderson, B. (2004). *The growth of YouthBuild: A case study.* Retrieved from http://www.caseatduke.org/documents/youthbuilddec2003case.pdf

Guillen, M., & Garcia-Canal, E. (2009). The American model of the multinational firm and new multinationals from emerging economies. *Academy of Management Perspectives, 23*(2), 23–35.

Habisch, A., Meister, H. P., & Schmidpeter, R. (2001). *Corporate citizenship as investing in social capital.* Berlin, Germany: Logos.

Hakanson, H. (1982). *International marketing & purchasing of industrial goods: An interaction approach.* Chichester, England: John Wiley.

Hambrick, D. C., & Mason, P. A. (1984). Upper echelons: The organization as a reflection of its top managers. *Academy of Management Review, 9,* 193–206.

Hamel, G., & Prahalad, C. K. (1985). Do you really have a global strategy? *Harvard Business Review, 63*(4), 139–148.

Hannan, M. (1998). Rethinking age dependence in organizational mortality: Logical formalizations. *American Journal of Sociology, 104,* 126–164.

Hansen, E. L. (1995). Entrepreneurial network and new organization growth. *Entrepreneurship: Theory & Practice, 19*(4), 7–19.

Hansmann, H. (1987). *Economic theories of nonprofit organization.* In W. W. Powell (Ed.), *The nonprofit sector: A research handbook* (pp. 27–42). New Haven, CT: Yale University Press.

Harding, R. (2004). Social enterprise: The new economic engine? *Business Strategy Review, 15*(4), 39–43.

Harding, R. (2009). *Social Entrepreneurship Monitor 2006.* Retrieved from http://www.deltaeconomics.com/media/Socialentrmon2006.pdf

Harding, R., & Harding, D. (2008a). Interview with Liam Black, CEO of Fifteen. *Social Entrepreneurship in the UK.* Retrieved from http://www.deltaeconomics.com/media/social2008fullreport.pdf

Harding, R., & Harding, D. (2008b). Interview with Sev Necati of Women & Young People's Safety Solutions. *Social Entrepreneurship in the UK.* Retrieved from http://www.deltaeconomics.com/media/social2008fullreport.pdf

Harding, R., & Harding, D. (2008c). Interview with Sheetal Mehta of Shivia. *Social Entrepreneurship in the UK.* Retrieved from http://www.deltaeconomics.com/media/social2008fullreport.pdf

Harding, R., & Harding, D. (2008d). *Social Entrepreneurship in the UK.* Retrieved from http://www.deltaeconomics.com/media/social2008fullreport.pdf

Hardy, K. (1986). Key success factors for small/medium sized Canadian manufacturers doing business in the United States. *Business Quarterly, 51*, 67–73.

Harrigan, K. R. (2001). Strategic flexibility in the old and new economies. In M. A. Hitt, R. E. Freeman, & J. S. Harrison (Eds.), *Handbook of strategic management* (pp. 97–123). Oxford, England: Blackwell.

Hart, D. (1984). The virtuous citizen, the honorable bureaucrat and "public administration" [Special issue]. *Public Administration Review*, (44), 111–120.

Hartigan, P. (2006). It's about people not profits. *Business Strategy Review, 17*(4), 42–45.

Henton, D., Melville, J., & Walesh, K. (1997). *Grassroots leaders for a new economy*. San Francisco, CA: Jossey-Bass.

Herbst, K. (2004). *How to change the world: First step toward becoming a social entrepreneur*. Retrieved from http://www.changemakers.net/journal/04february/index.cfm

Herman, R., & Redina, D. (2001). Donor reactions to commercial activities of nonprofit organizations: An American case study. *International Journal of Voluntary and Nonprofit Organizations, 12*(2), 157–169.

Hill, C. W., Hwang, P., & Kim, W. C. (1990). An eclectic theory on the choice of international entry mode. *Strategic Management Journal, 11*, 117–128.

Hitt, M., Bierman, L., Uhlenbruck, K., & Shimizu, K. (2006). The importance of resources in the internationalization of professional service firms: The good, the bad, and the ugly. *Academy of Management Journal, 49*(6), 1137–1157.

Hitt, M., Hoskisson, R. E., & Ireland, R. D. (1994). A mid-range theory of the interactive effects of international and product diversification on innovation and performance. *Journal of Management, 20*, 297–326.

Hitt, M. A., Hoskisson, R. E., & Kim, H. (1997). International diversification: Effects on innovation and firm performance in product diversified firms. *Academy of Management Journal, 40*(4), 767–798.

Hitt, M. A., Lee, H., & Yucel, E. (2002). The importance of social capital to the management of multinational enterprises: Relational networks among Asian and Western firms. *Asia Pacific Journal of Management, 19*, 353–372.

Hirschman, A. O. (1958). *The strategy of economic development*. New Haven, CT: Yale University Press.

International Franchise Association. (2009). *International Franchise Association: Frequently asked questions about franchising*. Retrieved from http://franchise.org/industrysecondary.aspx?id=10008

It takes a village. (2009). *Industrial Engineer, 41*(1), 13.

Jacob-Scharli, N. (2001). *William Browder: Ready for battle*. Retrieved from http://specials.ft.com/davos2001/FT3RY777DIC.html

Jacob-Schanli, N., & Murray, P. (2001) *Iqbal Quadir: Idle moments lead to rural revamp*. Retrieved from http://specials.ft.com/davos2001/FT3NODGJBIC .html

Jaffee, D. (2001). *Organization theory, tension and change*. New York: McGraw-Hill.

Jensen, M. C. (1986). Agency costs of free cash flow, corporate finance and take-over. *American Economic Review, 76*, 323–329.

Jenssen, J. I., & Koenig, H. F. (2002). The effect of social networks on resource access and business start-ups. *European Planning Studies, 10*(8), 1039–1046.

Johanson, J., & Vahlne, J. E. (1977). The internationalization process of a firm: A model of knowledge development and increasing foreign market commitments. *Journal of International Business Studies, 8*, 23–32.

Johanson, J., & Vahlne, J. E. (1990). The mechanism of internationalization. *International Marketing Review, 7*(4), 11–24.

Johanson, J., & Weidershiem-Paul, F. (1975). The internationalization of the firm: Four Swedish cases. *Journal of Management Studies, 12*, 305–322.

Jolly, V. K., Alahuhta, M., & Jeannet, J. (1992). Challenging the incumbents: How high technology start-ups compete globally. *Journal of Strategic Change, 1*, 71–82.

Jones, M. (1999). The internationalization of small high-technology firms. *Journal of International Marketing, 7*(4), 15–41.

Jones, C., & English, J. (2004). A contemporary approach to entrepreneurship education. *Education + Training, 46*, 416–423.

Julien, P. A., Joyal, A., Deshaies, L., & Ramangalahy, C. (1997). A typology of strategic behavior among small and medium sized exporting business: A case study. *International Small Business Journal, 15*, 33–49.

KaBOOM. (2009). *About KaBOOM*. Retrieved from http://kaboom.org/ WhoWeAre/FundingPartners/tabid/102/Default.aspx

Kalantaridis, C. (2004). Internationalization, strategic behavior, and the small firm: A comparative investigation. *Journal of Small Business Management, 42*(3), 245–262.

Kanter, R. (1999). From spare change to real change: The social sector as beta site for business innovation. *Harvard Business Review, 77*, 122–133.

Karakaya, M., & Stahl, M. J. (1991). *Entry barriers and market entry decision*. New York: Quorum Books.

Kaynak, E., & Kothani, J. (1984). Export behavior of small and medium sized manufacturers. *Management International Review, 2*, 61–69.

KickStart. (2009). *About KickStart*. Retrieved from http://www.kickstart.org

Kim, L. (1997). *Imitation to innovation: The dynamics of Korea's technological learning*. Boston, MA: Harvard Business School.

Kim, W. C., Hwang, P., & Burgers, W. P. (1993). Multinationals' diversification and the risk-return trade-off. *Strategic Management Journal, 14*, 275–286.

Kingdon, J. W. (1984). *Agendas, alternatives, and public policies*. Boston, MA: Little, Brown.

Kiva. (2009). *About Kiva*. Retrieved from http://www.kiva.org

Knight, G., & Cavusgil, T. (1996). The born global firm: A challenge to traditional internationalization theory. *Advances in International Marketing, 8*, 11–26.

Kogut, B. (1991). Country capabilities and permeability of borders. *Strategic Management Journal, 12*, 33–48.

Kogut, B., & Singh, H. (1988). The effect of national culture on the choice of entry mode. *Journal of International Business Studies, 19*(3), 411–432.

Korosec, R., & Berman, E. (2006). Municipal support for social entrepreneurship. *Public Administration Review, 66*(3), 448–462.

Kotha, S., Rindova, V., & Rothaermel, F. (2001). Assets and actions: Firm specific factors in the internationalization of U.S. Internet firms. *Journal of International Business Studies, 32*(4), 769–791.

Kotler, P., & Armstrong, G. (1999). *Principles of Marketing*. Upper Saddle River, NJ: Prentice-Hall.

Kramden. (2009). *About Kramden*. Retrieved from http://www.kramden.org

Kuemmerle, W. (2002). Home base and knowledge management in international ventures. *Journal of Business Venturing, 17*(2), 99–122.

Kwok, C. C. Y., & Reeb, D. M. (2000). Internationalization and firm risk: An upstream-downstream hypothesis. *Journal of International Business Studies, 31*(4), 611–629.

Larson, A. (1992). Network dyads in entrepreneurial settings: A study of the governance of exchange relations. *Administrative Science Quarterly, 37*(1), 76–104.

Leadbeater, C. (1997). *The rise of the social entrepreneur*. London, England: Demos.

Leadbeater, C., & Goss, S. (1998). *Civic entrepreneurship*. London, England: Demos.

Lechner, C., & Dowling, M. (2003). Firm networks: External relationships as sources for the growth and competition of entrepreneurial firms. *Entrepreneurship & Regional Development, 15*, 1–26.

Lecraw, D. (1977). Direct investment by firms from less developed countries. *Oxford Economic Papers, 29*, 445–457.

Lee, A. (2009). *Acumen fund*. Retrieved from http://www.fastcompany.com/magazine/131/the-acumen-fund-portfolio-data-management-system.html

Lee, H., & Park, J. (2006). Top team diversity, internationalization and mediating effect of international alliances. *British Journal of Management, 17*(3), 195–213.

Lee, K., & Kwok, C. C. Y. (1988). Multinational corporations vs. domestic corporations: International environmental factors and determinants of capital structure. *Journal of International Business Studies, 19*, 195–217.

Letts, C., Grossman, A., & Ryan, W. (1999). *High performance nonprofit organizations: Managing upstream for greater impact.* New York: Wiley.

Light, P. C. (2008). *The search for social entrepreneurship.* Washington, DC: Brookings Institution Press.

Lissner, J. (1977). *The politics of altruism: A study of the political behaviour of voluntary agencies.* Geneva, Switzerland: Lutheran World Federation.

Locke, R. M. (2002). *Note on corporate citizenship in a global economy.* MIT IPC Working Paper 02-009. Cambridge, MA: Industrial Performance Center, MIT.

Lu, J. W., & Beamish, P. W. (2004). International diversification and firm performance: The s-curve hypothesis. *Academy of Management Journal, 47*(4), 598.

Madhok, A. (1997). Cost, value, and foreign market entry mode: The transaction and the firm. *Strategic Management Journal, 18*(1), 39–61.

Madhok, A., & Tallman, S. D. (1998). Resources, transactions and risks: Managing value through interfirm collaborative relationships. *Organization Science, 9*, 323–339.

Madsen, T. K., & Servais, P. (1997). The internationalization of born globals: An evolutionary process? *International Business Review, 6*(6), 561–583.

Maignan, I., & Ferrell, O. C. (2000). Measuring corporate citizenship in two countries: The case of United States and France. *Journal of Business Ethics, 23*, 283–297.

Manlova, T. S., Brush, C. G., Edelman, E., & Greene, P. G. (2002). Internationalization of small firms: Personal factors revisited. *International Small Business Journal, 20*(1), 9–31.

Mars, M., & Garrison, S. (2009). Socially oriented ventures traditional entrepreneurship education modes: A case review. *Journal of Education for Business, 84*(5), 290–296.

Marschan-Piekkari, R., Welch, D., & Welch, L. (1999). In the shadow: The impact of language on structure, power and communication in the multinational. *International Business Review, 8*(4), 421–440.

Matthews, J. A. (2006). Dragon multinationals. *Asia Pacific Journal of Management, 23*, 5–27.

McDougall, G. (1991). Small New Zealand business and exporting: Some observations. *New Zealand Journal of Business,* 107–116.

McDougall, P. (1989). International versus domestic entrepreneurship: New venture strategic behaviour and industry structure. *Journal of Business Venturing, 4*(6), 387–400.

McGirt, E. (2009). *Enterprise community partners.* Retrieved from http://www.fastcompany.com/magazine/131/edward-nortons-9000000000-housing-project-thats-9-billion.html

McLeod, H. (1997). Cross over. *Inc., 19*(7), 100–104.

Medbank. (2009). *About Medbank.* Retrieved from http://www.medbankmd.org

Meyer, J. W., & Rowan, B. (1977). Institutionalized organizations: Formal structure as myth and ceremony. *American Journal of Sociology, 83,* 340–363.

Michael, A. (2006). *Securing social enterprise's place in the economy.* Retrieved from http://www.sbs.gov.uk/sbsgov/action/news

Miller, J., & Pras, B. (1980). The effects of multinational and export diversification on the profit stability of US corporations. *Southern Economic Journal, 46*(3), 792–805.

Mitchell, A., Shaver, M., & Yeung, B. (1992). Getting there in a global industry: Impacts on performance of changing international presence. *Strategic Management Journal, 13,* 410–432.

Monti, J. A., & Yip, G. S. (2000). Taking the high road when going international. *Business Horizons, 43*(4), 65–72.

Mort, G. S., Weerawardena, J., & Carnegie, K. (2003). Social entrepreneurship: Towards conceptualization. *International Journal of Nonprofit and Voluntary Sector Marketing, 8*(1), 76–88.

Mugler, J., & Miesenbock, J. (1986). *Determinants of increasing export involvement of small firms.* International Council of Small Business Proceedings World Conference, 189–205.

Murray, P. (2001). *Fields Wicker-Miurin: Distinguished alumni takes stock.* Retrieved from http://specials.ft.com/davos2001/FT3LWXE7DIC.html

National Foundation for Teaching Entrepreneurship. (2009). NFTE. Retrieved from http://www.nfte.com

Nike. (2009). *Nike vision statement.* Retrieved from http://www.nike.com

Norvell, W., Andrus, D. M., & Gmalla, N. V. (1995). Factors related to internationalization and level of involvement in international markets. *International Journal of Management, 12*(1), 63–77.

O'Hanlon, C. M. (2001). *Ted Halstead: Searching for a new America.* Retrieved from http://specials.ft.com/davos2001/FT3ZNSI7DIC.html

Olson, M. (1965). *The logic of collective action.* Cambridge, MA: Harvard University Press.

O'Reilly, C., Snyder, R., & Boothe, J. (1993). Effects of executive team demography on organizational change. In G. Humber & W. Glick (Eds.), *Organizational change and redesign: Ideas and insights for improving performance* (pp. 147–175). New York: Oxford University Press.

Oster, S. M. (1995). *Strategic management for nonprofit organizations: Theory and cases*. New York: Oxford University Press.

Overholt, A., Dahle, C., & Canabou, C. (2004). Social capitalists. *Fast Company, 78*, 45–57.

Oviatt, B. M., & McDougall, P. P. (1994). Toward a theory of international new ventures. *Journal of International Business Studies, 25*, 45–64.

Oviatt, B. M., & McDougall, P. P. (2005). Defining international entrepreneurship and modeling the speed of internationalization. *Entrepreneurship Theory & Practice, 29*, 537–553.

Pakes, A., & Ericson, R. (1998). Empirical implications of alternative models of firm dynamics. *Journal of Economic Theory, 79*, 1–45.

Papadopolous, N. (1988). Inventory, taxonomy, and assessment of methods for international market selection. *International Marketing Review, 5*(3), 38–51.

Paquet, G. (1997). States, communities and markets: The distributed governance scenario. In T. J. Courchene (Ed.), *The Nation-state in a global information era: Policy challenges the Bell Canada Papers in Economics and Public Policy 5* (pp. 25–46). Kingston, Ontario: John Deutsch Institute for the Study of Economic Policy.

Parker, P. (2008). *The 2009–2014 World Outlook on Franchising*. CA: ICON Group International, Inc.

Parkinson, C., & Howorth, C. (2008). The language of social entrepreneurs. *Entrepreneurship & Regional Development, 20*(3), 285–309.

Partners in Health. (2009). *About Partners in Health*. Retrieved from http://www.pih.org/home.html

Paton, R. (2003). *Managing and measuring social enterprises*. London, England: Sage.

Pearce, J. (2003). *Social enterprise in any town*. London, England: Calouste Gulbenkian Foundation.

Peng, M. W., & Heath, P. (1996). The growth of firms in planned economies in transition: Institutions, organizations, and strategic choice. *Academy of Management Review, 1*, 492–528.

Petersen, B., Welch, D. E., & Welch, L. S. (2000). Creating meaningful switching options in international operations. *Long Range Planning, 35*(5), 688–705.

Pharoah, C., Scott, D., & Fisher, A. (2004). *Social enterprise in the balance*. Glasgow, England: Charities Aid Foundation.

Philanthropic Initiative. (2000). *What's a donor to do? The state of donor resources in America today*. Retrieved from http://www.tpi.org/_tpi/promoting/research.htm

Plunley, D. J. (2000). *Global e-commerce: The market, challenges, and opportunities*. Irvine, CA: Bowne Global Solutions.

Pomerantz, M. (2003). The business of social entrepreneurship in a "down economy." *In Business, 25*(2), 25–28.

Porter, M. E. (1985). *Competitive advantage: Creating and sustaining superior performance.* New York: Free Press.

Porter, M. E. (1990). *The competitive advantage of nations.* New York: Free Press.

Post, J. E. (2000). *Meeting the challenge of global corporate citizenship.* Boston, MA: Boston College Center for Corporate Community Relations.

Pozorski, C. (2000, Fall). Social venture partners: "Venture capital" grantmaking in practice. *Grantmanship Center Magazine*, 24–26.

Prahalad, C. K., & Hamel, G. (1990). The core competence of the corporation. *Harvard Business Review, 68*(3), 79–91.

Prahalad, C. K., & Hart, S. L. (2002). The fortune at the bottom of the pyramid. *Strategy + Business, 26*, 2–14.

Pronk, J. (2002). *Economy in the service of life.* Retrieved from http://64.233.161 .104/search?q=cache:sDmHEG5BDuQJ:www.stichtingoikos.nl/rtf/report _consultation.rtf+Russel+Botman+solidarity&hl=en

Puttnam, D. (2004). Hearts before pockets. *New Statesman, (17)* 793, 26.

Reeb, D., Kwok, C. Y., & Baek, Y. (1998). Systematic risk in the multinational corporation. *Journal of International Business Studies, 29*, 263–279.

Reis, T., & Clohesy, S. (1999). *Unleashing the new resources and entrepreneurship for the common good: A scan, synthesis and scenario for action.* Battle Creek, MI: W. K. Kellogg Foundation.

Renzulli, L. A., Aldrich, H., & Moody, J. (2000). Family matters: Gender, family, and entrepreneurial outcomes. *Social Forces, 79*(2), 523–546.

Reuber, A. R., & Fischer, E. (1997). The influence of management team's international experience on the international behaviors of SME's. *Journal of International Business Studies, 28*, 807–825.

Reynolds, J. (2008). *IFA Franchising Modes.* Interview with S. Bleyer, D. Gwinnel, M. Kamikawa, & E. Maurice. Retrieved from http://www.communitywealth .com/CWV%20Capstone%20Team%20Findings%20Report%20--FINAL %20--%2024%20Apr%2009.pdf

Reynolds, P. D., Hay, M., Bygrave, W. D., Camp, S. M., & Autio, E. (2000). *Global entrepreneurship monitor: 2000 executive report.* Kansas City, MO: Kauffman Center for Entrepreneurial Leadership.

Rhyne, E. (2005). Maintaining the bottom line in investor-owned microfinance organizations. *Microbanking Bulletin, 11*, 13–17.

Rockwood, K. (2009a). *Academy for Urban School Leadership.* Retrieved from http://www.fastcompany.com/magazine/131/the-academy-for-urban-school -leadership.html

Rockwood, K. (2009b). *DataDyne.* Retrieved from http://www.fastcompany.com/ magazine/131/datadyne-episurveyor.html

Rogerson, C. M. (2004). The impact of the South African government's SMME programmes: A ten-year review (1994–2003). *Development South Africa, 21*(5), 765–784.

Roth, K. (1992). Implementing international strategy at the business unit level: The role of managerial decision-making characteristics. *Journal of Management, 18*(4), 769–798.

Rugman, A. M. (1981). *Inside the multinationals: The economics of international markets.* London, England: Groom Helm.

Rui, H., & Yip, G. S. (2008). Foreign acquisitions by Chinese firms: A strategic intent perspective. *Journal of World Business, 43,* 213–226.

Salamon, L. M. (1993). The marketization of welfare: Changing non-profit and for-profit roles in the American welfare state. *Social Service Review, 67*(1), 16–39.

Salamon, L. M. (1997). *Holding the center: America's nonprofit sector at a crossroads.* Retrieved June 16, 2009, from http://www.ncf.org

Sanders, W., & Carpenter, M. A. (1998). Internationalization and firm governance: The roles of CEO compensation, top team composition, and board structure. *Academy of Management Journal, 41,* 158–178.

Sapienza, H., Autio, E., George, G., & Zahra, S. (2006). A capabilities perspective on the effects of early internationalization on firm survival and growth. *Academy of Management, 31*(4), 914–933.

Sarkar, M. B., Cavusgil, S. T., & Aulakh, P. S. (1999). International expansion of telecommunications carriers: The influence of market structure, network characteristics and entry imperfections. *Journal of International Business Studies, 30,* 361–382.

Scholte, J. A. (2000). *Globalization: A critical introduction.* Basingstroke, England: Palgrave.

Servaes, H. (1996). The value of diversification during the conglomerate merger wave. *Journal of Finance, 51*(4), 1201–1225.

Shane, S. (1994). The effect of national culture on the choice between licensing and direct foreign investment. *Strategic Management Journal, 15,* 627–642.

Shapiro, A. (1986). *Multinational financial management.* Boston, MA: Allyn & Bacon.

Shokay. (2009). *About Shokay.* Retrieved from http://www.shokay.com/article01.asp?KindID2=23

Shore, B. (2009). *Streams of hope: Social franchising—a new path to wealth for nonprofits.* Retrieved from http://www.communitywealth.com/Streams%20of%20Hope.pdf

Slater, S. F., & Narver, J. C. (1995). Market orientation and the learning organization. *Journal of Marketing, 59,* 63–74.

Smallbone, D., & Wyer, P. (1995). *Export activity in SMEs.* Center for Enterprise and Economic Development Research, Working Paper Series, No 9.

Snyder, R.C. (1999). *Shutting the public out of politics: Civic republicanism, professional ethics, and the eclipse of civil society.* Dayton, OH: Occasional Paper of the Kettering Foundation.

Social Enterprise Alliance. (2009a). *Social entrepreneurship profile—Brooklyn Justice Counsel (PTBA).* Retrieved from http://www.se-alliance.org/case_studies/6_2005.pdf

Social Enterprise Alliance. (2009b). *Social entrepreneurship profile—Canadian Society of Association Executives (PTBA).* Retrieved from http://www.se-alliance.org/case_studies/1_2003.pdf

Social Enterprise Alliance. (2009c). *Social entrepreneurship profile—Community Catalyst (PTBA).* Retrieved from http://www.se-alliance.org/case_studies/9_2004.pdf

Social Enterprise Alliance. (2009d). *Social entrepreneurship profile—Food Share Toronto (PTBA).* Retrieved from http://www.se-alliance.org/case_studies/2_2004.pdf

Social Enterprise Alliance. (2009e). *Social entrepreneurship profile—Mill Center at Dixon Hill (PTBA).* Retrieved from http://www.se-alliance.org/case_studies/12_2003.pdf

Social Enterprise Alliance. (2009f). *Social entrepreneurship profile—NFTE (PTBA).* Retrieved from http://www.se-alliance.org/case_studies/11_2003.pdf

Social Enterprise Alliance. (2009g). *Social entrepreneurship profile—Strategic Employment Solutions (PTBA).* Retrieved from

Social Enterprise Alliance. (2009h). *Social entrepreneurship profile—Sylvan Beach Case (PTBA).* Retrieved from http://www.se-alliance.org/case_studies/2_2005.pdf

Social Enterprise Alliance. (2009i). *Social entrepreneurship profile—Teacher Support Network (PTBA).* Retrieved from http://www.se-alliance.org/case_studies/3_2004.pdf

Social Enterprise Alliance. (2009j). *Social entrepreneurship profile—Vision Support Trading (PTBA).* Retrieved from http://www.se-alliance.org/case_studies/4_2005.pdf

Social Enterprise Reporter. (2009). *About Social Enterprise Reporter.* Retrieved from http://sereporter.com

Spreitzer, G. M., McCall, M. W., & Mahoney, J. D. (1997). Early identification of international executive potential. *Journal of Applied Psychology, 82,* 6–29.

Steensma, H. K., Marino, L., Weaver, M., & Dickson, P. H. (2000). The influence of national culture on the formation of technology alliance by entrepreneurial firms. *Academy of Management Journal, 43,* 951–973.

Suchman, M. C. (1995). Managing legitimacy: Strategic and institutional approaches. *Academy of Management Review, 20,* 571–610.

Sullivan, D. M. (2007). Stimulating social entrepreneurship: Can support from cities make a difference? *Academy of Management Perspectives, 21*(1), 77–78.

Svetlicic, M., Jacklic, A., & Burger, A. (2007). Internationalization of small and medium enterprises from selected Central European economies. *Eastern European Economics, 45*(4), 36–65.

Tallman, S., & Fladmoe-Lindquist, K. (2002). Internationalization, globalization, and capability-based strategy. *California Management Review, 45*(1), 116–135.

Tallman, S., & Li, J. T. (1996). Effects of international diversity and product diversity on the performance of multinational firms. *Academy of Management Journal, 39*, 179–196.

Teach for America. (2009). *About Teach for America.* Retrieved from http://www .teachforamerica.org

Teece, D. J. (1986). Transaction cost economics and the multinational enterprise. *Journal of Economic Behavior & Organization, 7*, 21–45.

Teece, D. J., Pisano, G., & Shuen, A. (1997). Dynamic capabilities and strategic management. *Strategic Management Journal, 18*(7), 509–533.

Ten Thousand Villages. (2009). *About Ten Thousand Villages.* Retrieved from http://www.tenthousandvillages.com

Terjesen, S., O'Gorman, C., & Acs, Z. (2008). Intermediated mode of internationalization: New software ventures in Ireland and India. *Entrepreneurship & Regional Development, 20*(1), 89–109.

Thaler, R. H., & Sunstein, C. R. (2008). *Nudge.* New Haven, CT: Yale University Press.

Theobald, R. (1987). *The rapids of change: Social entrepreneurship in turbulent times.* Indianapolis, IN: Knowledge Systems.

Thompson, J. (2002). The world of the social entrepreneur. *International Journal of Public Sector Management, 15*(5), 412–431.

Thompson, G. F. (2005). Global corporate citizenship: What does it mean? *Competition & Change, 9*(2), 131–152.

Thompson, J., Alvy, G., & Lees, A. (2000). Social entrepreneurship: A new look at the people and the potential. *Management Decision, 38*, 328–338.

Tracey, P., & Phillips, N. (2007). The distinctive challenge of educating social entrepreneurs: A postscript and rejoinder to the special issue on entrepreneurship education. *Academy of Management Learning and Education, 6*(2), 264–271.

TROSA. (2009). *About TROSA.* Retrieved from http://www.trosainc.org/program/index.htm

Tuckman, H. P., & Chang, C. (2004). Commercial activity, technological change, and non-profit mission. In W. W. Powel & R. Steinberg (Eds.), *The non-profit sector: A research handbook.* New Haven: Yale University Press.

Tyson, L. D. A. (2004). *Good works—with a business plan.* Retrieved from http://www.businessweek.com/magazine/content/04_18/b3881047_mz007.html

Uzzi, B. (1997). Social structure and competition in interfirm networks: The paradox of embeddedness. *Administrative Science Quarterly, 35*(42), 35–67.

Vahlne, J. E., and Nordstrom, K. A. (1993). The internationalization process: Impact of competition and experience. *International Trade Journal, 7*(5), 529–548.

Vermeulen, F. (2001). Controlling international expansion. *Business Strategy Review, 12*(3), 29–36.

Vermeulen, F., & Barkema, H. (2001). Learning through acquisitions. *Academy of Management Journal, 44*, 457–476.

Vernon, R. (1966). International investment and international trade in the product cycle. *Quarterly Journal of Economics, 80*(2), 190–207.

Vilaga, J. (2009a). *Hopelab.* Retrieved from http://www.fastcompany.com/magazine/131/hopelab-video-games-for-health.html

Vilaga, J. (2009b). *Institute for One World Health.* Retrieved from http://www.fastcompany.com/magazine/131/the-institute-for-oneworld-health.html

Vilaga, J. (2009c). *Mercy Corps.* Retrieved from http://www.fastcompany.com/magazine/131/mercy-corps-the-bank-of-banks.html

Waddock, S. (2001). The multiple bottom lines of corporate citizenship: Social investing, reputation, and responsibility audits. *Business and Society Review, 105*, 323–345.

Waddock, S. A., & Post, J. E. (1991). Social entrepreneurs and catalytic change. *Public Administration Review, 51*(5), 393–401.

Wallace, S. (1999). Social entrepreneurship: The role of social purpose enterprises in facilitating community economic development. *Journal of Developmental Entrepreneurship, 4*, 153–175.

Weisbrod, B. A. (1998). Institutional form and organizational behavior. In W. W. Powell & E. S. Clemens (Eds.), *Private action and the public good* (pp. 69–84). New Haven, CT: Yale University Press.

Weiss, A. M., & Anderson, E. (1992). Converting from independent to employee salesforce: The role of perceived switching costs. *Journal of Marketing Research, 29*(1), 101–115.

Welch, L. S., & Luostarinen, R. (1988). Internationalization: Evolution of a concept. *Journal of General Management, 14*(2), 34–55.

Wellman, B. (1999). *Networks in a global village.* Boulder, CO: Westview.

Westhead, P., Wright, M., & Ucbarasan, D. (2001). The internationalization of new and small firms: A resource-based view. *Journal of Business Venturing, 16*, 333–358.

Whitelock, J., & Munday, P. (1993). Two cases in the industrial explosives industry. *Journal of International Marketing, 1*(4), 19–30.

Wilken, P. H. (1979). *Entrepreneurship: A comparative and historical study.* Norwood, NJ: Ablex.

Wilson, H. (2000). Internationalization of small and medium-sized enterprises (SMEs). In M. Tayeb & M. Harlow (Eds.), *International business theories, policies and practices* (pp. 198–220). United Kingdom: Pearson Education.

Wong, P. L., & Ellis, P. (2002). Social ties and partner identification in Sino-Hong Kong International Joint Ventures. *Journal of International Business Studies, 33*(2), 267–289.

Woolcock, M., & Narayan, D. (2000). Social capital: Implications for theory, research, and policy. *The World Bank Observer, 15*(2), 225–249.

World Economic Forum. (2002). *Global corporate citizenship: The leadership challenge for CEO's and boards.* Davos, Switzerland: World Economic Forum.

World of Good. (2008). *World of Good.* Retrieved from http://www.worldofgoodinc.com/about/index.php.

World of Good. (2009). *About World of Good.* Retrieved from http://www.worldofgood.org

Wrigley, N., & Currah, A. (2003). The stresses of retail internationalization: Lessons from Royal Ahold's experience in Latin America. *International Review of Retail, Distribution & Consumer Research, 13*(3), 221–243.

Young, M. (1997). Do-gooders with savvy. *New Statesman, 126*(1), 20.

Young, D. R. (2002). The influence of business on nonprofit organizations and the complexity of nonprofit accountability. *American Review of Public Administration, 32*(1), 3–19.

Young, D. R., & Salamon, L. M. (2002). Commercialization, social ventures, and for-profit competition. In L. M. Salamon and D. R. Young (Eds.), *The state of non-profit America,* (pp. 423–446). Washington, DC: Brookings Institution Press.

YouthBuild. (2009). *About YouthBuild.* Retrieved from http://www.youthbuild.org/site/c.htIRI3PIKoG/b.1223921/k.BD3C/Home.htm

Zadek, S., & Thake, S. (1997). Send in the social entrepreneurs. *New Statesman, 26,* 31.

Zahra, S. A., & George, G. (2002). International entrepreneurship: The current status of the field and future research agenda. In M. A. Hitt, R. D. Ireland, S. M. Camp, & D. L. Sexton (Eds.), *Strategic entrepreneurship: Creating a new mindset* (pp. 255–288). Oxford, England: Blackwell.

Zahra, S. A., Ireland, R. D., Gutierrez, I., & Hitt, M. A. (2000). Privatization and entrepreneurial transformation: Emerging issues and a future research agenda. *Academy of Management Review, 25,* 509–524.

Zander, A. (1993). *Making boards effective: The dynamics of nonprofit governing boards.* San Francisco: Jossey-Bass.

Zhao, H., & Luo, Y. (2002). Product diversification, ownership structure, and subsidiary performance in China's dynamic market. *Management International Review, 42*(1), 27–49.

Zott, C. (2003). Dynamic capabilities and the emergence of intraindustry differential firm performance: Insights from a simulation study. *Strategic Management Journal, 24,* 97–125.

Index